P9-DEW-950

the parrot who thought she was a dog

Nancy Ellis-Bell

The Parrot who thought she was a Dog

Harmony Books
New York

The names and identifying characteristics of some individuals have been changed to protect their privacy.

Published in the United States by Harmony Books, an imprint of the Crown Publishing Group, a division of Random House, Inc., New York.
www.crownpublishing.com

Harmony Books is a registered trademark and the Harmony Books colophon is a trademark of Random House, Inc.

Library of Congress Cataloging-in-Publication Data
Ellis-Bell, Nancy.
The parrot who thought she was a dog / Nancy Ellis-Bell.—1st ed.
1. Macaws—California—Anecdotes. 2. Pet owners—California—Anecdotes. 3. Ellis-Bell, Nancy. I. Title.
SF473.M33E45 2008
636.6'8650929—dc22 2007047952

ISBN 978-0-307-40594-4

Printed in the United States of America

Design by Elina D. Nudelman

10 9 8 7 6 5 4 3 2

First Edition

To Sarah, who flies forever free,
and the spirit of my mother who flies with her

the parrot who thought she was a dog

I LEAVE NO TRACE OF WINGS IN THE AIR,
BUT I AM GLAD THAT I HAVE HAD MY FLIGHT

—*Rabindranath Tagore*

CHAPTER 1

WHEN I ARRIVED home from New York, the massive black cage dominated most of our small living room. Looking out from behind the bars was the blue-and-gold macaw that my friend Samantha had given me without cost because of my track record in redeeming problematic or rescue animals. "Peg Leg," as she had been named by her previous owner, was a rescue bird, much larger than I remembered and, according to her previous veterinarian, vicious. I had seen her only once at Samantha's wild bird rescue ranch, but here in our ten-by-twelve-foot space she seemed far more imposing. She was nearly two feet tall, and her most impressive feature was certainly her feathers, brilliant blues and golds that extended to the tip of each two-foot wing. Then there were the eyes, soft black inside a white mask streaked with black lines like those of a Mayan shaman or African warrior. The effect was dramatic and not just a little intimidating, although not as intimidating as the beak, also black, which from nose to crown measured nearly four inches. She had only one foot. Her left foot had been cut off by her captors while they tried to release her from the parrot snare that had ended her life as a free bird in the Amazon basin. As I moved closer to the cage, her powerful gaze asked only one question: Predator or prey?

The bird I had originally wanted was an African grey, far smaller than a macaw and known for its high verbal fluency and mild temperament. I had first seen one at a "Parrot Weekend Experience" sponsored by Samantha and a group of breeders, rescuers, owners, and veterinarians. For three days I listened to lectures, heard amazing stories of bird antics and adventures, while interacting with both domestically raised and wild-caught parrots—from cherry-headed conures to cockatoos to African greys to the ultimate macaw, the largest of all the parrots and the most temperamental. Given the size of the macaw's beak and the bird's propensity for biting, I was hesitant to hold one or have it perch on my arm. Much more my style was the grey I fancied, who unfortunately already belonged to someone else. This weekend had been a gift from my husband, Kerry, who thought I would enjoy being exposed to these exotic creatures far beyond my usual family of dogs and cats. Something happened during that weekend, some strange pull to these living relics from the dinosaur age who seem to know what we have forgotten about being wild and wise.

When I was a child, lost animals always seemed to find me—mostly cats and dogs but sometimes hamsters or guinea pigs. When I was six, I had a gopher friend for whom I would steal carrots from the refrigerator, then sneak outside to feed him in his burrow. Even after I became an adult, cats and dogs still gravitated to me, along with the occasional squirrel or raccoon. When I met Kerry, my family was small—one dog and one cat—but I warned him that more would show up; it was only a matter of time. Since our home is in the woods, the possibilities were endless. I'd recently rescued a baby squirrel who had fallen from its tree home and landed in the middle of our deck, where my numerous cats were circling for the kill. Wrapping him in a fluffy washcloth, I carried him in a sling that held him against my chest for warmth and a friendly heartbeat. I fed him mashed-up fruits, along with a little water, and he slowly regained his strength. After a few days, I took him to a stand of oak trees whose branches offered many possibilities for both a new home and safety from marauding cats.

But I had never owned an exotic animal, believing firmly that wild things belong in wild places. Peg Leg brought the point home. There in her five-by-four-foot cage, her wings could not fully extend to their nearly four-foot span. In the jungle from which she came, she would have flown above the leafy canopy, following air currents down to the river to take a drink or bathe. She was now somewhere between four and six years old, having been captured when she was approximately two. She had not flown or bathed in all that time. The method of her capture is no less sad. Although illegal today, the preferred method of capture has been parrot snares or nets, placed to trap unwary birds. In her case, the left foot became hopelessly tangled in the mesh and her captors were forced to cut off her left foot in order to release her. From there she had been shipped to a first-time breeder in Nebraska who had illusions of raising scores of little birds that would sell for as much as two thousand dollars each. The illusion didn't take account of the incessant screaming of two macaws who hated each other and refused to mate. In retaliation and frustration, the woman beat them with a stick poked through the bars. Saddened by her own behavior, the woman offered the birds to a local veterinarian who had contacts in California for wild bird rescues. Peg Leg and her mate then made their way to Samantha who added them to her other sixty or so birds, all wild-caught and all living in cages. Her aviary was under construction when I attended the Parrot Weekend, but even when completed it would be able to accommodate only fifteen to twenty birds; the rest would remain caged and, to my mind, spiritually broken. Peg Leg's scenario was even worse; she was sick with an infectious disease, so her cage was in isolation in a tiny laundry room. That was where I first met her.

When I had left for New York, I was not yet convinced that I could or would trade my African grey dream for a macaw nightmare. Kerry had offered to buy me a grey, planning to have the bird there for me when I returned. Still, there was something about Peg Leg's eyes that captivated me from our first meeting; that proud bird in a pitiful cage was beginning to unravel my dream. I told Kerry that I would leave the final decision up to him, since he was going to have to live with the bird, too. Both he and I agreed that birds should not be caged, so the temperament issue was crucial. Peg Leg was vicious, trying to bite whoever fed her through the bars. Was this a bird we could live with? What about our other animals—and those to come? What would happen if things didn't work out and we had to return her to Samantha? What to do, what to do?

We said yes.

CHAPTER 2

We had to give Peg Leg a new name. She was a beautiful bird, a proud and fearless bird, a bird of grace. Peg Leg would never do. Kerry suggested "Sarah" because he thought it was a beautiful name. I agreed, because in Hebrew the name means "princess" and I thought she was one.

"Hello, Sarah; you are such a beautiful bird."

Over and over I repeated those words, rhythmically erasing the terrible sound of "Peg Leg." Even our two dogs, Ben and Blanco, seemed somehow reassured by the sound of her name coming from me, the one they loved and who fed them so well. Ben had been our first dog together after I moved onto Kerry's property. A rescue dog, he had been abandoned by his owners and wandered for months during the winter out on the road beyond our place. Taken to the Barking Lot, a local rescue facility for dogs and cats, he found himself in the caring hands of Audrey, who spent nearly two months stripping his badly matted fur. Mostly Tibetan Terrier, he looked nothing like his elegant heritage when I saw him in his dog run. "Last on the right," he had been with Audrey for six months; no one wanted to adopt him because he wasn't cute enough with his buzz-cut black-and-white body. It's always about the eyes. I looked at him, and we both knew. I named him Bentley, which soon became Ben, and I called him my little Buddha dog because he was so mellow and wise-looking. If Ben was Buddha, Blanco was Attila the Hun. Nicknamed Blanco the Killer Maltese Terrier, he was pure white and feared nothing—not other dogs, not cats, not raccoons, not deer, not even the occasional bear.

Our two house cats, Mr. Mistoffelees and Tiger, had bolted for the great outdoors when the cage arrived. Mistoff the Magnificent was far too diffident to care about another animal unless it encroached upon his food or petting time. Tiger was a rescue cat from our local McDonald's, where he had been fattening himself into fast-food obesity. When the cats did eventually saunter back inside, they looked up at the cage with a certain curiosity but not any kind of concern. As they say, "cage bars make good neighbors."

For several hours, I sat on the daybed across from the cage, reading and intoning my macaw mantra. I added that I loved her, even if I couldn't be sure that it would ever be true. I had never tried to love a creature whom I might never be able to touch or to share affection with. And the book I had bought didn't address how to rehabilitate a vicious bird; there mustn't be many humans who try. This was all new territory, and there were bound to be many mistakes. I only hoped none would involve the loss of a digit.

As dinnertime approached and Kerry was due to return from work, I went over to Sarah's cage to check on her food situation. All cages have swing-out dishes that lock from the outside. The challenge with a vicious bird is that it will try to bite you when you are opening or closing the gates. Kerry had devised a way to open the food dish door without jeopardizing a finger: a small metal "blocking plate" with a center-mounted knob that blocked the open gate while food or water was being dispensed, then raised as the dish went back into place. She still had plenty of food, but I decided to experiment with putting nuts through the bars directly into the dish. I'd have to be quick, but I knew I had to start building a relationship with Sarah. This was a good place to start.

I brought gifts for the goddess from the kitchen: almonds, walnut halves, and one peanut. With their high oil content, peanuts are very dangerous for birds as excessive oil can kill them. Birds should also never eat avocado or chocolate.

"Hi, Sarah; you're such a beautiful bird, and I love you. Would you like some nuts?"

I don't know if anyone else had offered her nuts; Samantha's bird diet was nut-free. Time to find out. Sarah watched me as I moved my hand toward the food dish; she didn't move one inch. Only her eyes followed my movements; hands, after all, were her enemies.

"Treats for Sarah, treats for Sarah." The word *treat* must have cross-species universality because all of my animals have understood that word immediately.

She still hadn't moved, so I cautiously, fearfully, tossed an almond into the dish. Then a walnut half, more almonds, and finally the peanut. She still didn't move. I backed away from the cage and moved onto the daybed to see what she would do. Nothing. This might be harder than I thought. I decided to look away and feign interest in something else. After a few very long seconds, I noticed, out of the corner of my eye, Sarah moving very slowly sideways on her perch toward the treats. Success! The peanut went first, and as I turned my head to watch more closely I could see her pupil become a pinpoint of excitement. When she had finished all the nuts, she swooshed her beak back and forth in the dish. It looked to me like a little bit of happiness.

Maybe, just maybe, this would work.

CHAPTER 3

DESPITE SAMANTHA'S WARNING that Sarah could scream loud enough to make a human chest vibrate, she had not done so with me. The telephone call that changed everything was from an editor who was making me an offer on a new book. Sarah was quiet, and I listened as the editor outlined the preliminary terms. The advance was less than I had hoped for, and my voice must have reflected that disappointment. Before I could respond . . .

"Crap! It's crap!"

"What?" she asked. "What you you mean it's crap?"

"No, no," I assured her. "I didn't say it was crap, the bird did!"

"The bird? What do you mean, the bird?"

I explained that I had just acquired a macaw, that my separate office cottage wasn't yet ready (my husband was the contractor), and that I was handling my business calls in the house—with a bird that I hadn't known had any vocabulary skills, until now. She laughed. Still, the disappointment in my voice when she made a slightly higher offer did not go unnoticed.

"Bummer, it's a bummer!"

What? How many other words did Sarah know? Had she been captured by a group of hippies whose lingo would now punctuate my every day?

I groaned; the editor laughed again.

"Well," she said, "I've never done business with a bird before. Will she be overseeing the contract negotiations as well?"

We ended our conversation in laughter, and I turned to Sarah, who had now become quiet as the proverbial mouse. She gave me a look that said in no uncertain terms, "That's only the beginning."

The "beginning" extended to liberal use of "crap," "bummer," and "bad bird"—all expressed in her best earsplitting voice and always at the most unexpected moments. Feeding time in particular became an adventure.

"Kerry, would you please feed Sarah? It's nearly thirty minutes later than what she's used to, and I'm trying to talk on the phone."

With me, she would lower her head slowly to one side, then to the other, while I fed her. I learned that this is a sign of affection and "equality" among macaws, and I was delighted. She stopped trying to bite my hand when I fed her, and I was able to abandon the metal plate, which Kerry still had to use. Mostly I fed her, but he fed her on an occasional basis so that she would be accustomed to him when I was on business trips. For him, that little shield was a necessity. His antics reminded me of the three hundred Spartans up against the Persians, shields held strategically in place. Most of the time it worked, but Sarah was a clever little Persian and he was sustaining battle wounds. Beyond that, she had no interest in him. All macaws choose one mate, and that's it. I was in; Kerry was out. He accepted that she was my bird and gave up on having any kind of intimate relationship with her.

"Crap, crap, crap!"

My head was starting to throb, and I was catching only one word out of every two or three from my client.

"Bad bird, bad bird!"

There was that chest vibration that Samantha had warned me about, and my temper index was rising.

"Kerry!" Now I was screaming, which only made Sarah scream louder. I ended my call and decided to feed her myself. The idea of uncaging her was now paramount. Perhaps that would soothe her frustration.

Kerry and I had been discussing when to let her out of her cage. That decision would be final; once she was uncaged, it would be impossible to get her back into the cage unless she wanted to go. Most macaws will step up onto your arm and let you place them wherever you choose, including back into their cages. Sarah couldn't be touched for any reason, and Samantha had suggested we wait for that very reason. I had become convinced that it was time.

"Okay, hon; I can't take much more of this. What do you think about uncaging her now?"

"We might as well find out what we've gotten ourselves into."

We were ready. We chose a Saturday morning to release our new friend; that way, we'd have the weekend to monitor what she would do without the interruptions of business calls. Whatever it was, we were ready to find out. Once she was freed, all bets were off. Time to gamble.

I walked over to the cage and once again told her how beautiful she was and how much I loved her. I put my hand on the cage door, inches away from her beak and claw. She didn't move, her eyes fixed not on my hand but on my face. I began to unscrew the clamp that secured the door lock. Macaws are notorious for unlocking their cages, so savvy owners employ back-up mechanisms. She didn't move, her gaze still fixed on my face. I removed the clamp. I lifted the arm and slid it back through the groove. All that remained was to open the door. She still hadn't moved, only now her gaze had dropped to the cage door. I pulled the door open, swinging it back so that there was no obstruction to her release. Again she didn't move. Her eyes became pinpoint pupils, a sure sign of agitation or surprise. I stepped back a few feet and spoke the words that would forever change my life.

"You're free, Sarah; you're free."

She climbed out of her cage.

CHAPTER 4

NOTHING in what I had been told or had read prepared me—or my dogs—for the carnivorous aspect of macaws. Phase one of the avian surge was food, followed by phase two: water.

When most people think of birds, they think seeds and nuts. Sarah's diet while caged was predominantly organic bird kibble, occasional nuts, and fresh fruits and vegetables. She loved bananas, liked apples, hated all citrus. Once I offered her mangoes and papayas, thinking these would remind her of home. Not her home. Right to the bottom of the cage they went. Her favorite vegetable was anything crunchy with water inside; celery was her top choice. All of our animals are fed an organic diet, liberally augmented by special treats like Greenies and beef or lamb rib bones. The dogs are grateful for all blood protein.

From what I understood, greys, cockatoos, and conures were not so keen on meat products, but a certain lack of information exists when it comes to the raptor quality of macaws. I would later find out from other macaw owners that, unlike the ones kept by Samantha (herself a vegetarian), their birds loved meat, especially lamb and chicken.

The first indication that Sarah was indeed one of these little flesh eaters occurred on her second day of freedom. The first day had been very quiet. She had left the top of her cage only to come down and eat. Kerry had secured the food and water gates in an open position, so she did not have to return to her cage to dine or drink. I could hardly sleep during the first few days she was uncaged, anxious for the slightest sound of trouble. There wasn't any. The next morning, she was perched as she had been during the day, her head turned 180 degrees to rest between her wings.

Ben and Blanco were already at their food dishes. They were eager for the two beefy rib bones I had placed next to their kibble. By now Sarah had climbed down to her food dishes, which I had replenished with her usual breakfast. She noodled her beak back and forth deep into the pellets and nuts, spraying them out of the dish onto the floor. Ben's interest in his bone temporarily shifted to the morsels on the floor. It was an unfortunate shift. In a matter of seconds, Sarah launched herself off the cage and headed straight for his kibble and bone. She was about to initiate new house rules.

RULE 1: NO KIBBLE OR BONE IS SACRED

Sarah screamed, and both dogs bolted for safe ground, Blanco with his bone in tow, Ben leaving his behind. First she stuck her head into their food, scrambling it from side to side as she had done with her own food. Every now and then she would take a bite, looking most satisfied with her newly expanded diet. The dogs looked at me for support; I was clueless. Should I feed her dog food?

RULE 2: BIRDS DO EAT BONES

The kibble wasn't enough; now she wanted the bone. This was no short rib; this was a full-blown rib, which had to weigh nearly as much as she did. I would later learn that macaws' hauling strength matches that of ants. For now, I watched in disbelief as she climbed back up to the top of her cage, bone tightly clamped between her beak and crop, the lower part of her jaw. Despite her missing foot and claw, she maneuvered her other foot and the tip of her beak to navigate the bars. Once on top, she held the bone in her claw like a weight lifter doing curls. She explored it with her tongue, and then *crack!* The bone had not been her goal; it was the prized marrow inside. Again using her tongue, she licked and extracted every particle until the bone was clean. A quick drop to the floor, and the bone once again became Ben's. He picked it up and walked over to a corner of the living room to gnaw happily.

RULE 3: WATER RIGHTS ARE NONNEGOTIABLE

Now she was thirsty. Back down the cage she went and over to their water dish, a heavy piece of crockery six inches deep and almost two feet across. She dipped her beak, drank, drank again, and tipped her head to one side as if on the brink of an idea. Birds love water; they love to bathe all over to the point of being drenched. Sarah tested the edge of the dish for stability and climbed up. She immersed her entire head, tossed it back, and struck a pose of both surprise and delight. Birds will bathe only in water they can drink. Once the water passed muster, she was in. All the way in. For nearly twenty minutes she dunked, splashed, and chortled while the dogs watched in horror. Would nothing be sacred for them anymore? Her bathing complete, she climbed out looking like a winged rat, climbed back up on her cage, and groomed herself for nearly an hour. It was a sweet moment; it must have been the first bath she'd had since before she was captured.

My vision of what a macaw companion would be was undergoing radical revision. There was going to be competition with the dogs for their food. There was going to be an ongoing mess—bird food on the floor, dog food on the floor, gallons of water on the floor, and of course prodigious amounts of bird poop. This was not going to be a bird who gazed at me lovingly while she nibbled an almond in silence. I began to realize that for all I had read, for all those discussions at the Parrot Weekend, for all that I thought I knew, Sarah was not a bigger version of the parakeet we'd had when I was growing up. I was back in the Pleistocene era; I had adopted a raptor. There was also going to be noise, lots of noise.

CHAPTER 5

I HAD SEEN Sarah eyeing the dogs' toy basket. A large, broad-handled basket, it was filled with well-marked and saliva-saturated stuffed animals, rubber squeezies, ropies, assorted balls, and chew toys.

Macaws love toys, and I had festooned her cage, inside and out, with all varieties of bird accessories. She found them interesting but not significant, and by week three she was on the search for new entertainment. Macaws are easily bored, moving like a three-year-old from one toy to the next. Eventually, a human three-year-old grows up. Macaws may live to be eighty years old, but their attention span is stuck at toddler.

Fortunately, the dogs were outside when Sarah climbed up on the basket for the first time. Her pupils narrowed, then expanded, full to her lashed rims; if her beak were physically capable of a smile, there would have been one curving somewhere between whimsy and malice. Her first target was a small stuffed bear—Ben's favorite—with dark brown fur, a plastic nose, and hard button eyes. Ben was not a destructive dog, so the face was intact. By contrast, Blanco's stuffed toys had been immediately rendered faceless.

The eyes were the first to go. Then went the nose and a large portion of its abdomen. Fluffy intestines spilled to the floor. Within minutes, the bear was an empty sack. I had been so mesmerized by Sarah's methodical dismemberment that I had watched, motionless, as she destroyed it.

Now having tasted blood, she buried her head among the survivors. Back up on the deck, the dogs were looking in through the glass doors at the bitch in their basket. Four eyes looked at me for justice. I snapped back into consciousness.

"No, Sarah, no! Those aren't yours. No, no!" I waved my hand over the basket as if it were some kind of magic bird wand. I swear she laughed.

I picked up an ostrich-feather duster. For reasons I still don't understand, she hated that thing and would immediately retreat if I produced it as a diversion from whatever mischief she was currently engaged in. I had discovered this by accident while using it to rid the house of cobwebs. No sooner had I snared a web only a couple of feet from the top of her cage than Sarah withdrew to the window side of the cage, her pupils large and her wings outstretched. Not realizing I had startled her, I went after the next web more slowly, but with the same result for Sarah. It was an *Aha!* moment for me. Since I had no idea how to discipline or dissuade an uncaged bird who couldn't be touched, the feather duster became my salvation. It couldn't possibly hurt her, so I felt humane in using it.

Deprived of her booty but bear-satisfied, she climbed back up onto her cage. The dogs came running back inside to assess the damage. Ben sniffed the fur carcass and looked at me for an explanation. I hugged him, told him what a good dog he was, and bought him a new bear the next day. Sarah, on the other hand, knew she had won another victory in her house takeover. She'd routed the dogs. Was I next?

More important, what kind of limits did I need to set? Kerry's only concern was that Blanco might attack her. He'd never had a pet, so he had no concept of territorial toys. And like many fathers, I suppose, he was leaving discipline up to me. As long as the bird wasn't chewing up his things, he was fine. But I sensed that little bears were only the beginning of avian domination and destruction.

CHAPTER 6

THE TOY BASKET had to be protected, and I had to make clear decisions about limits. So far, Sarah had confined her travels to the living room and the front part of the kitchen, where the dog dishes were located. Why should I think that she would be content with those boundaries forever? It was only a matter of time until she pushed her way into the kitchen itself and eventually the bedroom. Besides, she was now beginning to follow me wherever I went, including the kitchen. I went into the bedroom only at night, when Kerry was home, and I folded laundry on top of the daybed so as to keep a better eye on her. Time to think like a bird.

I sat down on the living room floor and looked around. What would I see if I were only two feet tall? What would be most intriguing? Sarah looked at me from the top of her cage. Surely she was wondering what I was up to. Opportunities and limits began to present themselves to me. Under the daybed were storage boxes and part of Kerry's record collection. Cardboard, vinyl, disaster. In the corner behind the daybed was a tangle of cords and wires that were the life force of the living room.

No power, electrical shock.

A Victorian tabaret with open shelves, family treasures on display. Devastation.

My Hepplewhite credenza with its brass hardware and gold leaf moldings. Except for the handles, the surface was smooth. Was it climbable? Chewable? If chewable, what about the lead in the paint?

Destruction and death. And I hadn't even left the living room.

Into the kitchen I went, Sarah still watching from the top of her cage. She didn't go into the kitchen unless I was there, but I had to believe that at some point she would. Down on the floor, I surveyed a very different kitchen from the one I observed standing up. Since all cabinets were open, the first two feet held lots of temptations: foodstuffs, cans, dog food, cat food, pots, cleaning products, the garbage can, and our propane line.

Gas leak. Explosion. More death.

I was feeling overwhelmed. When my friends with children had lamented how hard it was to childproof their houses, I had smiled as if I understood their predicament. At least their children would grow up someday. I would just have to be logical and discuss everything with Kerry. Time to return to the daybed and pretend I was in New York in my wonderful hotel suite overlooking the Hudson, where the red-tailed hawks Pale Male and Lola live *outside* the buildings.

A few moments into my paperwork and calls, I noticed Sarah climbing down off her cage and toward the daybed. She had never tried to climb up the daybed; household domination is clearly an ongoing process.

"Hi, Sarah. Mommy's busy with work." I had been using the words "busy" and "work" with the dogs, who understood that these words meant they weren't going to get any attention from me. Sarah had been free less than a month and up to this point had been busy with her own "work."

I sat cross-legged, looking down at her as she studied the architecture of her next adventure. The bottom frame of the daybed was too high for her to reach, even on tippy-claw. The legs were two-by-twos and might just be climbable. Sure enough. Using her beak for pull and her foot for push, she was up with me in a nanosecond. Once there, she did her little side-to-side head motion, and I responded.

"Good girl, Sarah, good girl! What a smart bird you are!"

Was I crazy? Praising her for an accomplishment that might now empower her to see our house at many approachable levels! I quickly moved all the papers out of reach, along with the phone. She was obviously pleased with herself and began to explore the coverlet, pillows, and window ledge. The window ledge was wide enough for her to stand on and to get a direct view of the garden much better than the view from two feet. Her pupils went from tiny to large and back again. She raised her wings at the shoulders but close to the body, a sign of excitement and "power." Bobbing her head up and down, she was clearly pleased with herself. I got off the daybed to give her more room and to see what she would do. After a few minutes on the window ledge, she turned her attention to the coverlet and pillows. As if vacuuming with her beak, she rubbed it back and forth across the coverlet, ululating as she did so. This went on for several minutes; then she went for the pillows. At first, she only played with the tassels in her mouth, tonguing the silky strings from side to side. Tonguing soon turned to tugging, and I decided to retrieve the pillows before they lost anything of value. For several minutes more she played with the coverlet and looked out the window, obviously happy with her new perch.

Where was I going to sit from now on?

The issue of limits clearly had to be resolved sooner than later. I tackled those limits methodically. First I moved the toy basket to the top of the woodpile next to the woodstove. Only when I was in the room did I put it back on the floor. The woodpile held no interest for her so far; if it ever did, I would choose a new basket perch. Next I crawled under the daybed, bundled all the cords and wires, and pulled them up to the wall unit, where I tucked them in behind the television. Then I found a heavy blanket, which I placed over all the boxes under the daybed, folding the edges under strategic boxes. Finally I moved all the family treasures from the tabaret to the top shelves of the wall unit.

So far, so good.

The kitchen would require hours and hours of rearrangement, along with Kerry's help. I would think about that tomorrow. Meanwhile, I went into the bedroom to create my new office space. Sarah didn't follow me in, but I was no longer naive. Surely, in her brain, there was a thought similar to mine: "Tomorrow, I'll think about it tomorrow."

CHAPTER 7

TOMORROW brought a different focus from Sarah than the one I had expected. Instead of expanding her grounded world into the kitchen or bedroom, her new place of interest was the daybed. After having breakfast, both hers and the dogs', she ignored her other play choices and climbed right up on the daybed. I had already moved my papers into the bedroom, where I had converted the dresser top into a work shelf. The phone was with me all the time, and I preferred to make my calls from the daybed with its expansive light and serene view.

Given her comfy dais, Sarah was much quieter and less perturbed by my business conversations. She was content to look out the window and preen herself. Her grooming was incessant, and it gave me the opportunity to see her plumage more closely.

Macaws seen from a distance, flying in the wild or perhaps perched on a branch, reveal brilliant colors that incorporate every color of the rainbow. Blue-and-golds like Sarah combine blues that range from indigo to turquoise with golds that run from sunny yellow to burnished copper. Up close, as I was while sitting with her, I could see so much more.

First were the eyes, which reminded me of Theda Bara's, dark pupils set against a deep gold. Her eyes were ringed in black and rimmed with tiny black lashes that circled the entire eye. I had never seen an animal with such lashes. The feathers were no less amazing. All of them were to some degree iridescent and changed hue with the light. The shafts were the color of pearls and had their own type of luminescence. The skin beneath was so thin that I wondered how these birds could possibly keep warm. While her skin closely resembled that of a reptile, it wasn't actually scaly, and I wondered how it could withstand the constant biting that is typical of most parrots. The wings were a work of art in themselves. When she extended one to groom the feathers underneath, I could see the wing ribs that allowed her to fly. As she folded her wing back down, I could see the perfect alignment of one feather folding into the next. She was a marvel, all two pounds and two feet of her. Then I saw the evil dander.

With each feather tug came a flurry of infinitesimal dandruff, little puffs of white from just one feather. It was snowing! From three feet away the snow was invisible. Even when it lofted into the air, it was invisible—except to my lungs, which drew it in like a powdery magnet, coating my bronchial sacs in moist down. Since childhood I had experienced breathing difficulties. Some attributed it to a bronchial condition, some guessed asthma, some pointed to potential allergies; my vote was for two parents who smoked, including during my mother's pregnancy. I was sensitive to both cats and pollens, but our little parakeet had never been an issue, most likely because my father was the only one allowed to take him out of his cage. When free, he perched only on my father; I had never even been able to touch him.

Here with Sarah, I was facing a new problem. I found myself unable to take deep breaths. Since I talk for a living, this was a big issue. I also had trouble sleeping at night, despite the fact that I was in a different room. Both the bird veterinarian and my own physician came up with the same diagnosis: macaw dander. Apparently, people with breathing problems should not have birds at all. I was told to return the bird or live a "medicated" life. I was not going to live the rest of my life on drugs and inhalers. I had begun my academic career as a scientist, and I would do what any good scientist does when faced with a puzzling situation: analyze and resolve. My doctor prescribed me an inhaler, "just in case," which I never used. Kerry knew that when I set my mind on something, that was it. He was certainly concerned about my health, but I assured him that I had a plan.

As a child, our cat had caused me great misery. I was her feline couch, and my lungs paid the price. My parents, in typical 1950s fashion, did not believe in allergy medicines, and I was left to wheeze and sigh. When I left for college, my breathing became normal and stayed that way until Sarah arrived, despite the many cats I shared space with. My first apartment offered the ultimate solution. I had gotten a kitten, a blue-eyed, lilac-point Siamese whose fur shed constantly. I brushed, I combed, I bathed her. Then I had an inspiration: Perhaps if I had the kitten sleep with me, which was its first choice anyway, I could develop a quicker immunity through intense immersion. I would put up with a couple of miserable weeks that would force my body to develop its own defenses. I refused to consider the other possibility, then and now. It had worked then; it would work now.

Since Sarah did much of her grooming on the daybed, I used our intimate space to deal with the dander. Sometimes I would notice her staring at me, as if to ask "What *are* you looking at?" I just smiled. After two or three weeks, my breathing quieted down and I was once again able to enjoy the luxury of deep breaths. Sarah continued to preen, and I watched in loving awe. She had reminded me that no problem is insurmountable, regardless of what other people, including experts, say.

CHAPTER 8

SARAH'S TONGUE was a marvel in itself, more of a pedicle or "index finger" than a tongue, much like the famous finger of the alien in *E.T.* Food and climbing aside, it communicated her emotions. Birds, including macaws, kiss—with gusto. The term *French kiss* most certainly did not originate with the French; someone had a macaw. The more a macaw loves you, the more it will want to kiss you. Samantha had warned me that humans and birds should not kiss, not just because of the obvious bite issue but, more important, for health issues that could sicken the bird. With Sarah it wasn't an option. Feeding her, however, was our way of sharing "a kiss." If I offered her a grape, she would take it gently from my fingers, sweetly touching me with her tongue as she did so. Then she would first twirl it around with her tongue to be sure it was edible; macaws will not eat food that has passed its expiration date, unlike ravens, who have no such sensibility. When the grape passed muster, she would carefully skin it before eating the flesh inside. She did the same with pistachios, edamame, anything with a shell or skin. Those shells and skins became a significant part of the "macaw mess."

While I kept the cage and food surfaces clean, Kerry vacuumed daily. Our regular, heavy-duty vacuum was no match for shells and bone fragments, so Kerry had brought in the big gun: an industrial shop vacuum. Though perfect for the task at hand, it was too heavy for me to operate. He even installed a HEPA filter to help with the dust and dander. The reason I had fallen in love with Kerry was his unconditional, loving heart. I had never known anyone who could love that way, and it was the most seductive thing about him. It didn't hurt that he looks like a blend of Mel Gibson and Liam Neeson, but it was his beautiful soul that entranced me. When he saw how important Sarah was to me, he modified his schedule to make sure cleanliness was next to wifeliness.

The truth was that our house was being transformed into a cage. Aside from the cage itself, I had begun to create barricades of varying sorts to prevent Sarah from climbing or burrowing into places that harbored danger or destruction.

As one entered from the garden, which was struggling to bloom against the dull gray of the house, the woodstove sat directly across the room. In its original state it bore an iron sculpture of a roadrunner from my Arizona days, plus the occasional dish being warmed that sat on top. Now, to its left, stood a desperate dracaena surely wondering what kind of terrible karma had earned it a place right next to an inferno. Its purpose was to prevent Sarah from launching herself onto the stove from the woodbox. A few days earlier she had done just that. "Foot to the fire," she had stood unperturbed on the hot metal. I had been shocked. Didn't she feel pain? When I told Samantha, she assured me that macaw feet are exceedingly tough and can withstand a fair degree of heat. Still, I ushered her back to the woodbox and back down to the floor. That's when the hapless dracaena moved from the bedroom to the living room. It was an effective deterrent, too flimsy to support her weight, and she gave up on the woodpile.

To the right of the woodbox, itself a primitive effort at carpentry, was the lovely Hepplewhite credenza that in my previous home had been a proud member of my furniture family. Here it looked out of place with its ebony finish, gold-leaf moldings, and old-world brass hardware. I didn't think it looked like a climbing temptation with its flat surfaces.

RULE 4: IF IT'S THERE, SHE WILL CLIMB

Sarah must have been casing the piece for days, because when she began her ascent it was with a purpose that had to have been preceded by careful planning. Between beak and tongue, she raised herself up to the second brass pull, balancing with her foot on the first. Then, while perfectly balanced, she used her tongue to carefully unscrew the right side of the handle. Once removed, she played with it in her beak, then tossed it to the floor, ready for her next move. Out came the second screw, again to the floor. She continued to toss the screws as she ascended to the top of the credenza.

I was awestruck. Such balance, such ingenuity, such damage! Out came the feather duster, and down she went.

For a few days, she ignored the piece, but it was only a matter of time until she stripped the gold-leaf moldings. I put Vaseline on the remaining handles; it worked. She tried only once to grab one in her beak, and it took her nearly twenty minutes to wipe the goo off. It felt just a little cruel, but all the mess and destruction was making me a desperate woman. Now, every time I wanted to get into those drawers, I had to use a paper towel in order to grasp the pull myself.

To the other side of the woodstove was a large window that looked out onto the woodshed, one of Kerry's most artful constructions in post-and-beam style. In front of the window was my Victorian tabaret, which had already been emptied of its contents. In order to stop her from climbing and chewing that piece, I had covered it with a heavy African fabric that Sarah could not negotiate with only one foot.

Next to that was Sarah's cage, whose size made it second only to the daybed, thus helping to create a path through the living room that was roughly three feet wide, reminding me of that country-and-western song about love growing best in small places. That cowboy never paid a visit to our house. The few friends who came over stood slack-jawed at how we could live in such disarray and cramped conditions. There was no place to sit, and the fear of a flying pteradactyl kept our entertaining to the great outdoors.

On the facing wall were shelves that Kerry had built. As in the dresser in the bedroom, the bottom section of the cabinet was actually drawers that easily opened and closed. Kerry figured out how to thwart any attempts at accessing the contents by pulling a piece of wire across each drawer. Even a macaw can't chew through metal, so the drawers and shelves above were safe. The visual effect was jarring. At least the bedroom dresser looked normal.

Now we arrive at the daybed, where we had attached a bamboo screen as an additional climbing place for Sarah. Macaws cannot chew through bamboo, so the new perch was safe from strafing, but it also created additional problems.

With a small parrot, like a conure, the typical deposit of excrement is less than a third the size of a dime and odorless. With a macaw, morning drop aside, which approximates two tablespoons, the typical deposit is the equivalent of one teaspoon. The average macaw excretes dozens of times a day, and not all are straight, easy-to-clean drops. From the top of her cage, it was a clean hit to the "poop rug" waiting below. These were small washable rugs that were changed daily and that helped save the Oriental rugs beneath.

From the open door of her cage, or from the food and water gates, there were two drop possibilities: a clean hit to the floor if she arched her back sufficiently or a slider, which would cascade down the cage with a waterfall effect. From the top of the bamboo perch or any place on its climbing face, the slider was a given. At least she always aimed away from the daybed—or my head. Those were the only places she used, almost like a cat with two cat boxes.

Her poop also created an issue for the dogs, who already had a taste for the cat box. While my original dog, Kinder, had never developed such a taste, both Ben and Blanco were aficionados.

Consequently, we had weaned the cats off the box and encouraged them to go outside; problem solved. Exchange cat box for poop rugs. Changing those rugs was essential. It was also essential because a macaw "owner" needs to keep an eye on the color and consistency of excrement. "Healthy" is medium green with white streaks and is odorless. Digestive upsets (usually caused by foods that are too rich), which mean the diet needs to be modified, cause a browner color. Brighter green with minimal white indicates too much oil in the diet. Good poop plops; bad poop splats. I had become a scatologist.

CHAPTER 9

IT'S FUNNY how audible the sound of one foot can be. While I was on high alert for the living room, Sarah had been watching me retrieve laundry from the woodshed, which also housed our washer and dryer. In short order, there she was in the bedroom doorway, looking up at me with her head cocked to one side. Curiosity led to climbing, and up she came via the bedpost, which to this point had been distressed only by antique standards. I was proud of her ascent, despite the implications, and praised her handsomely for her feat.

"Good girl, Sarah; good girl! You are so smart!" Words of encouragement headed straight toward disaster.

Once on the footboard, she surveyed another new layer to her world. From a bird's-eye view, this room didn't hold much promise. Of course, there was the laundry basket.

I had continued to fold and stack and was roughly halfway through the task when Sarah decided she could be of help. First, she dove into the basket with the remaining clothes. Dove, literally, head first into the T-shirts, towels, sheets, and underwear. Maybe it was the combination of fabric and fabric softener, but the towels got her immediate attention. Using her beak like a scoop, she burrowed into the soft goods until her tail was straight up in the air. She was literally on her head in the middle of a bath towel. From there, the intoxication grew, spreading to sheets, T-shirts, and Oh, my God! my underwear. I am not a clotheshorse, but I love sensual underwear. It's what is closest to your skin, first thing on, last thing off. The leanings are definitely French. I line dry them, which is why they were in the bottom of the laundry basket.

So entranced was I watching Sarah enjoy her linen longings that I forgot, for the moment, what lay beneath. If the French kiss originated from a macaw's amorous pursuits, French lingerie must somehow be related. My favorite silk camisole soon became her personal favorite; it was too late to grab for it, lest it tear or be pierced by her beak. I didn't need to worry. Inexplicable as it sounds, she did nothing to harm the garment; instead, she tossed her head up and down as if she were waving the French flag. Then she blithely flung it over her head and I made a three-point catch. This continued with the rest of my underwear. I can only think that there was some intimate connection with those things that were "me." She continued to be my laundry helper from then on, burrowing for, shaking, and tossing the things that could touch me.

Sweet and special took a more sinister turn after several laundry basket encounters.

CHAPTER 10

THOUGH I WAS BEGINNING to have my doubts, Kerry still thought Sarah was sweet. That changed when she attacked his prize oak dresser in the bedroom. Since there was no laundry basket to beguile her this time, the climb up the bedpost gave her the opportunity to take a wider view of the room. I tried to think like a bird. What would catch *my* eye? Ah, a new Annapurna. There, only inches from the footboard, was Kerry's handmade oak dresser with its flush-mounted wood handles. Over the dresser were shelves holding family photographs and Kerry's bug collection, which had been carefully preserved in glass jars for easy viewing. When I awoke in the morning, I was greeted by the faces of my father and mother, both deceased, and the tiny faces, also deceased, of scorpions, spiders, tarantulas, and one bat. Would Sarah be intrigued by big bugs?

She climbed back down from the bed and stood directly in front of the dresser. There were four drawers on each side, placed directly next to each other. The workmanship was flawless, all grains matching, with drawers that pulled out like silk and closed just as smoothly. It, too, looked out of place in our forest retreat. I quickly assessed whether I should immediately go for the feather duster or just observe. My criterion for such decisions was simple: potential danger or destruction merited feathery rebuff. The tricky part was assessing what could be dangerous or destructive. Given the laundry basket and my underwear, I hadn't a clue as to the potential fate of the drawers' contents. If Sarah decided to tear and not toss, it would be too late to intervene with the duster, which was housed on a top shelf in the kitchen. Perhaps I should create a feather waist holster and look like an obsessive housekeeper. I was definitely flying in uncharted skies. Even books about macaws don't address such issues; their presumption is that owners will keep their birds caged.

My mind came back to the present situation. The way I saw the dresser was that the narrow wooden pulls would be too daunting; plus, they were spaced far enough apart to prevent her beak-and-tongue climbing technique. The living room dresser had bigger handles, ideal for climbing. Now she assessed the challenge. First she explored the lowest handle with her tongue and beak. So far, so good. Then she tried to reach for the second handle but couldn't reach it. So far, even better. Then she checked out the rim of the drawer. Uh-oh. Like a seasoned climber she balanced her foot on the handle and used her beak to grasp the rim and pull her body up—right up to the next handle. Such amazing ingenuity! In seconds she was to the top of the dresser, whose shelves above housed the bugs and photos. Those she could not reach. The dresser top itself was adorned simply with a silk runner—and my office papers. I executed my own rappeling maneuver and managed to sweep them out of reach and back down to the bed. I had already devised a more practical transfer scenario from dresser top to bed: the long, shallow cutlery drawer from my Hepplewhite credenza, which made moving all those papers quick and simple. Besides, the drawer served no purpose in our little house with no dining room; at least now it had a practical function.

What followed next had me laughing in a combination of hilarity and horror. There she was, looking down from her new perch, feeling very powerful. Head bobbing and wings lifted, she could have been on Everest. With the dresser scarf gone, what else could there be? She bent down her head until her beak touched the rim of the drawer. Because of its artful construction, it took only a slight nudge from her beak and the drawer opened fully, exposing a treasure chest of underwear—Kerry's, not mine. No doubt, if the underwear had been mine, I would have broken the hundred-yard dash record to retrieve the duster. Instead, I waited and watched.

First one sock, then another, then a pair of shorts. How would Kerry respond to this latest bird adventure? He wasn't at all fussy about his clothes; folding wasn't important, and ironing would have required that he own an ironing board, which he did not. Nor did I, for that matter. Sarah continued to toss socks out of the drawer. But not for long. Having tossed long enough, she decided it was time for diving. In she went, head first, tail up in the air, as she had done with the clothes in the laundry basket. Much like the chortle when she had discovered the dogs' water dish, she was gleeful as she began to toss other pieces into the air. When the drawer was finally emptied of its contents, she performed the most amazing feat of all.

While my new fear was that she might start chewing the drawer's edge, she had another plan in mind. She climbed to the outside rim and, as the drawer slowly began to close, she gingerly rappeled down to the next rim, then to the next, each drawer closing like silk above her until she reached the floor. Could there be a more amazing athlete? If there were some type of Olympics for birds, she would qualify in a heartbeat. Two or three sharp head thrusts told me she was proud of her achievement as well. She looked around at the tossed underwear, but it no longer interested her. It was time to check out the floor itself a little more carefully.

There was a certain fascination to her explorational antics. On the one hand, I was almost enchanted by her ability despite her missing foot. On the other, I was becoming more than just a little neurotic about what she would do next. I wanted to afford her all the freedom I possibly could, but the question remained: "When does her freedom encroach upon mine and Kerry's?" Or the other animals' for that matter? When is that line crossed? I had no answer. Each scenario was new, and decisions had to be made in the moment. I had the feeling I was being trained by a very clever mistress.

First she looked under the bed. Nothing there, just dust and the occasional spiderweb. Living in the country, I had grown accustomed to the occasional spider in the bed. I didn't need to fear black widows, which stayed hidden from humans; just those little "house spiders," which rarely bit. If they did, it was more like a mosquito bite and amounted to nothing. My greatest fear in terms of a bed hopper was the scorpion; and, yes, a scorpion would show up roughly once a year just to test my fear quotient. I've never been bitten by one under those circumstances; only once, outside in the garden, did a surprised fellow gently tap my foot so that I wouldn't step on him. The odds of a scorpion being under the bed at this moment were slim, so I wasn't worried about Sarah encountering one.

Having determined that there was nothing under the bed to interest her, she walked over to my side of the bed, where the dogs' beds were. These were their sacred places, safe from everything and the source of a good night's sleep. Sarah eyed Ben's bed, which was nearest to her. This time I knew just what to do. I sprinted for the kitchen and was back in the bedroom in seconds, feather duster in hand. Ben's favorite sleeping buddy was a squeaky toy, a purple dinosaur with bright green stripes. Maybe Sarah had primitive memories of her dinosaur heritage and wanted to test her raptor skills. By the time I returned, she was sniffing the little guy, and I stood, duster in hand, ready to strike. The sudden squeak startled her, and for the moment she dropped the toy. I lowered the duster, a strategic mistake. A quick reassessment, and she grabbed it again. Squeak! Squeak! Squeak! Silence. Her beak had already punctured the rubbery skin as I prodded her with the duster. A quick toss of her prey, and she grudgingly abandoned the dog bed to return to the living room.

Ben was going to be really upset. I hoped he would understand that this time I had tried to save his little friend. At least Sarah hadn't reached Blanco's stuffed rabbit. Ben was a forgiving creature; Blanco would hold a grudge. His choice of payback was to pee on one of my carpets, something Sarah hated as much as I did. If she walked over a wet spot, she would stop, put her beak to the source of the smell, shake her head, and walk around it. She did have certain sensibilities.

Now my own sensibilities were in question. Sarah had invaded the sanctum sanctorum—bed, dresser, dog beds. Kerry and I would need to reevaluate where her freedom stopped and ours was preserved. Time to test his limits of love for the woman who loved animals too much.

CHAPTER 11

"WE REALLY NEED a bigger house."

Kerry was tired and a little grumpy when he got home that night.

It was a lament I'd heard often, even before Sarah had arrived. Our little house is indeed "little," exactly forty-nine feet long and twelve feet wide, the size of a single-width trailer. It is in fact a little trailer that Kerry modified before he became a contractor and knew better. There is only one door—to the bathroom—and one can look from one end of the house to the other and get the "big picture." The bedroom is tiny, only ten by twelve, and houses a queen-size bed, two dressers, two dog beds, two nightstands, and exactly four horizontal feet of hanging, open-closet space for me. If I never bought another article of clothing, I might be able to squeeze my hangables into that space. As long as I didn't gain any appreciable weight, I would be able to navigate the twelve or so inches around the bed. The kitchen would require a photograph to do justice to its culinary injustice: a tiny stove salvaged from a motor home, no oven; yellow Formica countertops purloined from that same motor home; a pitted porcelain sink; open shelves everywhere; orange-striped wallpaper whose orange has been discolored by gas residue; and the cheapest of linoleum in the most garish "faux marble" pattern.

The bathroom gives the kitchen a run for its money, exactly five by six, with an even lower ceiling than the rest of the trailer, which topped out at a dizzying seven and a half feet. Of course, I overlooked all of this because it was the home I had come to when I fell in love with Kerry. I should also note that since I moved in the kitchen has been remodeled; the rest of the trailer is as it was when I arrived.

The house I left when I moved in with Kerry had three bedrooms, a chef-style kitchen, a formal dining room, a study, a large living room with fireplace, two bathrooms, and a garden that I had transformed into a tropical oasis. This, my "dream house," was a rental that I was hoping to buy. The house was in a suburb of San Francisco, and it was clear that Kerry could never live anywhere remotely urban; so our decision as a new couple was to build a new house on his property. Living in the trailer house would be temporary.

"Temporary" for a contractor has no expiration date, as I have come to understand and accept. I told Kerry when I met him that I would rather live with him in a small house than be on my own or with somebody else in a big house. So we continue to live in the small trailer house with birds, dogs, and cats while Kerry builds elegant, dramatic homes for others. I spend most of my time when Kerry is at work in my office cottage, which is a roomy 900 square feet with its own deck and brick patio. The ceilings are ten feet high, and windows abound. I hired my husband to build it. The bamboo flooring that I bought is still waiting to be installed, but I am grateful for this beautiful space.

"It's been nearly three years since I moved here," I added, "and I agree that a bigger house is essential. Perhaps you could start with clearing the site, then move on to the foundation . . ." He cut me off in midsentence.

"No. I want to take a year off and do nothing but build our house."

We'd had this discussion before, and it usually escalated into a mild argument: me trying to explain the difference between dream and illusion and he affirming that he would indeed build that house "someday." When other people wonder how or why he can put up with my animal adventures or with my expansive garden, which does not provide a single vegetable, only herbs, the answer is simple: compromise. The new house is the only raw nerve in our relationship, and both of us make a considerable effort not to work that nerve.

"Sarah explored the bedroom today, including your top drawer."

"Did she destroy anything?"

"No, she just tossed things around, but I refolded everything."

I then switched the conversation to his mother's long-promised visit. Even from hundreds of miles away, thinking of her brought things back to calmness.

That was it. Ruffled feathers had been smoothed. The house issue had been tabled for now, but the big bird issue remained. What to do about Sarah's endless explorations? Though she hadn't yet invaded the kitchen, we both knew it was just a matter of time. We didn't need to worry. She had other plans.

CHAPTER 12

SARAH HAD BEEN with us for nearly two months, uncaged for all but two weeks. In that time, she had carefully explored everything that started at ground level, working her way up to the top and always climbing back down. I was a little surprised that she hadn't tried to fly from one place to another. Her wings had not been clipped, even though that is common for most macaws in captivity. When we had taken her to see the vet for a checkup, he had asked if we wanted her clipped. Both Kerry and I had said no, not wanting to desecrate those magnificent wings. We also hoped that she would fly, exercising her wings so as not to develop the dreaded "wasting macaw disease." Caged birds with large wingspans are unable to fully extend their wings, let alone flap or fly with them. Such birds will not live to the optimal age of a free-flighted bird, nearly eighty years, but will likely die by the time they are ten to fifteen. The enzyme that in the wild allows them to beat their wings and stay airborne builds to deadly levels in a caged bird, literally emulsifying its muscles. It dies, unable to eat, drink water, or breathe. Sarah was not going to fall victim to that fate.

I knew her wings were perfect, and I knew she had flown when she was a wild bird. Part of me looked at our small space and wondered "How?" Another part wondered "Why not?" A smaller part said, "Maybe not." Ultimately, the decision was not ours. Once we let her out of her cage, the wing would be in her court. I was totally unprepared for the launch.

In the bedroom folding clothes, I was surprised that Sarah had not joined me there for her laundry ritual. She had stayed on top of her cage, seemingly content to know where I was. A sound like the wind from an oscillating fan was followed immediately by the landing of Sarah at the bedroom opening. Since our ceiling was only seven and a half feet high and her cage was five feet tall, she had had very little room from which to take flight. Somehow she had, and by the time she reached the bedroom she had knocked over only one lamp, miraculously sparing my childhood collection of ceramic horses. Because the bedroom opening was only three feet wide, she crashed to the ground just short of it. Collecting her dignity, she ruffled her feathers back into alignment and approached the bedpost with a new swagger. Her expression rivaled that of an Olympic gold medalist. To celebrate, she grabbed my French bra and waved it over her head, a new flag of victory.

I was ecstatic. "Sarah, Sarah, you flew!"

The head started to bob up and down and those wings rose higher than they ever had before. She knew. She remembered what it was to be a flying creature. She looked at me with an expression of appreciation for letting her be who she was. I couldn't wait to tell Kerry. Wait a minute—what about the dogs, the cats?

Everyone else had been outside when she launched, and she chose to walk back into the living room instead of flying. For the next couple of days she didn't fly at all. I didn't know why. I wondered if perhaps she had decided that our place was too small, her wings too big, and had resigned herself to being a ground bird.

On day three she took off again, this time from the bamboo screen straight into the kitchen. She landed on top of the butcher block cabinet, only taking out a full canister of French green lentils as she did. She looked around, and suddenly the concept of food emporium became a new reality. The counters were crowded with baskets of fruits, vegetables, nuts, and other chewables. Nothing was hidden from view. With her climbing ability, it was only a matter of time before she learned to access an endless bird buffet. I had to distract her.

At the same moment, Ben and Blanco had come into the kitchen from the bedroom, where they had been napping. When I walked quickly into the living room, right past them, they were more than a little concerned when she flew after me, directly over their heads. Ground attacks were one thing, but what were they supposed to do with a self-styled pterodactyl in their airspace?

She landed in the middle of the daybed. Her landing was more duck than flying diva, but she recovered her composure with a laugh. Macaws do have a sense of humor. They do little throat chuckles and they also laugh raucously, both at the appropriate moment. From "Heh, heh, heh" to "Ha, ha, ha," they know when the time is right. On this occasion, it was the former as she pulled her wings up and bobbed her head up and down. She was victorious again. I smiled back at her. "Heh, heh, heh."

RULE 5: WATCH YOUR HEAD

When a macaw is about to take flight, it lowers its head and points toward the desired landing space—or target. When the wings raise up in sync with the head, there are only seconds to get out of the way or take cover. I was in the bathroom when the dogs learned Rule 5. The first thing I saw was Ben scuttling toward the bedroom, tail tucked under. Then it was a double vision, Blanco barely making the safety of the bedspace with Sarah right over his back. She couldn't quite make the bed itself because her wings couldn't clear the bedroom opening. The dogs learned the lesson. Dive for cover, ideally in the bedroom; response time to escape harm, ten seconds.

It became Sarah's new game: strafe the terrier. Any chance she got, when she wasn't chewing heirloom furniture or casing the kitchen for treats, she would fly after Blanco. She never went after Ben. I think she respected his Buddha nature and saw him as something worthy of at least a little respect. No such luck for Blanco. His bravado was too much of a temptation. But even Blanco became adept at her signals. Most of the time it was Bird 0, Dog 1.

The cats' response was to live under the daybed or on the top shelf over the refrigerator. The angle was unworkable for Sarah's flying maneuvers; and their food was on top of the refrigerator anyway. They acted as if everyone lived with a flying monster and loved to look down on her.

Kerry's reaction to her flying powers was that we needed a bigger house. I just smiled.

CHAPTER 13

IN THE WILD, macaws have few natural predators because of their aerial existence. Certainly, a cat is not on their predator list, and Sarah carried that information with her to our little abode. Of the sixteen cats we had when she arrived, only two of them were indoor/outdoor cats. The one who had come with me into my marriage was Mr. Mistoffelees, named after the magical cat in the Broadway play *Cats.* He was indeed magical and very smart. He used his paws much like little hands and had a way of fixing his gaze in such a manner as to remind you that he was a leopard on the inside. He was semi-long-haired and defined as a "tuxedo cat," meaning black and white with a white chest and paws. He was magnificent. He was also haughty, and the arrival of the bird in no way fazed him—at first. The other cat was a rescue tabby who had been living as a beggar at the local McDonald's. We adopted him, spayed him, and switched him from fast food to healthy morsels, which included our reasonably healthy leftovers. We named him Tiger and the two cats became like brothers, grooming each other and sleeping together on the daybed—when the bird wasn't up there.

Cats in the wild do understand the concept of bird as predator. Large hunting birds can easily carry off one of their offspring or interrupt a kill. It's all about the beak and claws.

When the bird arrived and Kerry struggled to get the cage through the door opening, the cats didn't notice the bird at first. All they saw was a big metal monster invading their space, so they ran outside. Once it was in place, and after several hours of through-the-glass-smartly, they decided it was safe to return. Besides, it was time to eat and the food was inside. At first they just meandered into the kitchen and appraised the suitability of their current meal. Once satisfied, they ambled back into the living room for a nap atop the daybed. Now they saw the bird, leering at them from across the room. They looked at each other like two Disney cats; I half expected to see two bubbles of dialogue above their heads. Still, they didn't seem afraid; more thoughtful. They must have figured out that a bird in a cage is no problem. That, of course, had changed when I had let Sarah out of her cage.

Her first appearance as a free bird happened while they were outside purloining little mice and harassing little birds. When they came back in, she was on the daybed, where they couldn't see her at first. What they did see was an empty cage with an open door. Now they started to look around—and up. When she saw them, she moved to the edge of the daybed. She made only the slightest move and they were off, nearly tripping over each other as they ran for the bedroom. With the front door closed, it must have seemed like the only escape. For two days they did not leave the safety under the bed, disconcerting the dogs, who were now face to face with felines when they slept. Dutifully, I brought their food to them and placed a cat box next to the bed on Kerry's side, just in case they couldn't get outside. Cat poop, unlike bird poop, is nasty, as all cat owners will attest. I didn't need any more misplaced poop in my life.

As days turned into weeks, both cats came to accept her walking, then flying maneuvers. Occasionally she would chase them as they tried to get outside, nipping at their tails as they barely cleared the door.

The outdoor cats were a different matter, although I believe that both Mr. Mistoffelees and Tiger told big tales to their friends. We fed all of the outdoor cats on the deck, and Sarah soon figured out when it was feeding time. She would walk over to the sliding glass door and bang her beak against the glass, raising her wings as she did so. Given the eye level of a cat, that would make her appear to be nearly twice as tall as they were. Only hunger and their faith in glass eventually convinced them that they could eat safely. The indoor cats, on the other hand, had adjusted to having their food placed on top of the refrigerator, where the bird could not bother them. The outdoor cats eventually began to eat as they had before she arrived.

I always fed the cats around 6:00 P.M. so that they had plenty of time to come and go before our other family arrived. Even before most of the cats had joined our lives, Rachel had shown up. Rachel—as I named her—was a raccoon with four legs but only three feet. That "chew off their own foot to escape a trap" axiom may very well be true. In any case, I had begun to notice a raccoon coming up on the deck after dark, scavenging for any cat food pieces left lying about. I would sit on the other side of the glass door and watch; then I escalated to opening the door only a couple of inches so that she could hear my voice. Eventually, I opened the door wider, and ultimately I was able to sit with her while she ate. By now I was feeding her directly, adding vegetables and raw eggs, which she carefully "washed" before eating. I named her Rachel because I thought she was probably a good mother. After several months, she proved me correct when she brought her four pups with her to eat. While she had come to know and trust me—despite all my friends admonishing me about bites and rabies—her pups were unfamiliar with human smell and they barked. If I hadn't known better, I would have sworn they were dogs, hackling their back fur and baring their little teeth as they menaced me. By the time Sarah joined us, there were two generations of raccoons living under the house. They had torn out much of the insulation to create a warren effect, coming out to see us just when it was time to eat. The raccoons had only Sarah's image through the glass to contend with.

CHAPTER 14

While Sarah continued to spread her wings and explore the airspace in our house, Kerry and I retrofitted the kitchen to be less bird accessible now that she was flying there on a regular basis. To start, he installed cabinet doors on the shelves three feet from the floor. Since handles were an impossibility, he chose latches that secured from the top of each cabinet. These were the same kinds of latches we had used on our outside freezer, situated in the woodshed/laundry room. Despite its size and bulk, not to mention the hundreds of pounds of frozen food inside, a bear had managed to knock it over, exposing the iced treasures within. We had recovered most of its contents, but a few packages had disappeared, never to return. To preserve present and future foods, Kerry had lashed the freezer to the stalwart timbers and then installed four latches that could defy any marauding bear. These fortifications would also hold against our occasional mountain lion, the same one who later decimated our entire cat population except for Mistoff, Tiger, and the two outdoor cats who chose never to come inside despite our invitations. Of course, they had seen Sarah.

On the countertops we had exchanged baskets for sealable containers. Cleaning products and such were moved to the closed cabinets, along with animal foods. Appealing foods that could not be sealed were moved to shelves out of climbing reach. Dishes, pots, and baking pans stayed where they were. Sarah never seemed interested in them. Canned goods and spices were relocated to shelves out of climbing reach as well. The propane line was sheathed in metal and moved behind the stove. The kitchen was 90 percent bird safe. The rest we left to fate and the flyer.

The new issue—and with Sarah there was always a new issue—was the garden. From anywhere in the living room she could see me working outside. During winter, when I couldn't tend my plants, the garden was a nonissue; I wasn't out there and out of her presence. Now, seven months into her freedom flights, I was back outdoors working every chance I could. My evolving flower beds had grown out of a half acre, give or take, of small tan oaks, which are more like weeds and grew everywhere. They grew in the company of manzanita shrubs with their smooth red bark and madrones with their lime green bark "papered over" with red bark that peels into curls. At the twenty- to thirty-foot level were pin oaks, small conifers, firs, and pines. At the highest level were the larger firs and madrones, which could top 100 feet. I had cleared the area of anything under two feet tall and now had a canvas upon which I could build my serene space.

The total area for my new project was roughly one third of an acre. In two seasons, I had transformed the scrubby wasteland directly in front of the house, extending toward both the east and west into a garden of shrubs, botanicals, herbs, and exotics. Of course it wasn't enough.

In the area to the far east of the house was the stump of an impressive bay tree that measured beyond question twelve feet in circumference and nearly four feet tall. It was a venerable tree, and I wanted to honor it. Kerry was due to be gone for two months for a solar energy seminar in Colorado. Time to play.

I had been observing with chagrin a pile of bricks, easily three hundred of them, sitting right in the middle of my new garden space. I'd asked Kerry to move them elsewhere, but here they were after nearly two years. He hadn't been gone two days for his Rocky Mountain sojourn when I mobilized my plan to build a "yellow brick road" from the edge of the house to the bay tree stump, approximately forty feet long over uneven terrain.

I could carry only two bricks at a time, but I was on a mission. It took me three days of solid work to get within four feet of my goal. Those last four feet presented me with a new challenge: scorpions. Since childhood, I had been terrified of scorpions, and the fear had followed and stayed with me into adulthood.

There it was: a wood scorpion approximately three inches long, with a stinging tail that arched almost two inches over its back. What to do? It looked sleepy, but I wasn't taking any chances. I dropped both bricks and ran, my heart nearly beating out of my chest. I had a new crisis of faith: avoid the scorpion or finish the yellow brick road? I chose the path of the not-so-cowardly lion. I walked back over to the bricks armed with a five-foot-long fir branch with which I planned to sweep the scorpion out of human range. What if it could jump? Do scorpions jump? It was now or never. I swept the scorpion with enough force to catapult a small dog. It landed at least twenty feet away, and I took a deep breath. And another. What if there were more? It didn't matter. My adrenaline had turned me into Goliath, and the rest of the bricks made their way to that last four feet of walkway. I had won. But every victory has a caveat.

Sarah was more upset than ever that I was spending so much time outside working on the walkway. When I was working on the rest of the garden, I would come back inside at regular intervals and spend time with her. The walkway demanded that I not take breaks; once I broke the rhythm, the physical demands of what I was doing would stop me in my tracks. She was mad. When macaws are mad, they scream. She screamed.

Not short screams; screams that ran for twenty minutes or more. As it happened, a new neighbor had moved in across the street and was unaware of our bird stewardship. Later, he would sheepishly apologize for having caused such a fuss. But at the moment, and hearing what sounded like a woman screaming, he called the sheriff and reported what he thought was an incident of domestic violence.

It was nearly dark and Kerry was due home anytime, so I didn't find the approach of headlights up our road to be strange. Then came a second pair of headlights, then a third. My first thought was that something had happened to Kerry, and I went rushing down to the first vehicle, which was clearly a sheriff's SUV. Two officers quickly jumped out, hands on their guns, and immediately asked me if I was all right. I was so shocked that at first I couldn't speak. They repeated the question, and by now they were definitely looking around for some unseen perpetrator.

"I'm fine," I finally stuttered. "Is there a problem?"

"Yes, ma'am; we got a call of possible domestic violence, and we're here to make sure you're okay."

Domestic violence! Then the lightbulb flicked on: Sarah. Her screams, which sounded human, had caused someone to call the authorities. Now I faced a dilemma. If I told them the truth, that the screams were those of a bird, then in the future if something terrible happened when I really needed them, they would just say, "Oh, it's that weird woman with the big bird." So I opted for surprise and bewilderment.

"No, there's nothing wrong here. Whoever called you is mistaken. You're welcome to look around if you wish."

Ironically, they never went near the house. Instead, all six of them, hands on holsters, walked around the garden in search of an evil husband. One of them, the most aesthetic of the group, commented on the beautiful walkway. I thanked him for his compliment and went back into the house to confront the real perp. As the headlights all turned and left, I knew what she was thinking.

"You need to let me go outside."

CHAPTER 15

I COULDN'T POSTPONE my New York trip any longer; I needed to nurture my publishing roots and create new growth. Kerry was concerned. Could he deal with Sarah when I wasn't there? What if she became aggressive or severely depressed? What could he, should he do? How about his schedule? I was never more than a few hours, maybe one overnight away. This trip would last for ten days. Could he handle the extra responsibility? Could Sarah handle the separation?

I called Lori, my neighbor and dear friend, who had been caretaking my garden and looking in on the dogs when I traveled. She had been around Sarah on numerous occasions, and Sarah actually seemed to like her. Could she become a bird nanny in my absence?

"Hi, Lori. Listen, I'm wondering if you'd consider helping to take care of Sarah while I'm gone?" Her hesitation was short and the answer simple.

"Sure, Nan, I can help out. Just tell me what to do, and it won't be a problem."

That night, I told Kerry that Lori would be his helpmate with Sarah and that everything would be fine. I wanted to believe that; I needed to believe that. My business would be in jeopardy if I disappeared into the woods with my merry band of critters. Like a Manhattan "executive mom" who must at some point make a terrible decision about profession and motherhood, I was standing on a new threshold.

It was three days before I would leave and time to pack. Into the bedroom I went, Sarah right behind me. The suitcase was tucked under the bed where she had never seen it, and when I pulled it out she seemed hardly interested. When I set it up on the bed and opened it, everything changed.

Her head tilted to one side, she walked over to the edge of the bag and climbed up for a better look. "No laundry inside. Mmmm, how strange." I could just hear that bird brain working overtime.

"Sarah, Mommy has to go on a trip; not a little trip, a big trip; but Mommy will come home to you. Okay?" Previously, I had left for two short overnight trips to the Bay Area without any repercussions upon my return. I had intentionally left late in the day and returned in the late morning of the next day, and that time frame hadn't upset her. It helped, of course, that Kerry had modified his schedule so that she hadn't really been alone for more than an hour or two. This was different. Ten days were going to be a big test of our relationship. What if she became angry and reverted to her earlier viciousness? What if she became upset and then sick? Worst of all, what if my leaving caused her to reject me altogether?

While she stood on the edge, I began to fold my clothes and put them into the bag. She waited until the bag was nearly half full before she began to help with the packing process. Packing became unpacking as she grabbed blouses, skirts, and of course underwear and mightily tossed them onto the floor. This was not the gentle tossing reserved for the laundry basket; this was apparel war.

"Sarah, no, I need to pack those." Bra in beak, she demonstrated how much she wasn't listening. After several attempts to keep my clothes in the suitcase, I gave up in search of a better plan.

"Okay, Sarah, let's go get a treat! Come on, girl!" I was barely through the bedroom opening when there she was behind me, racing for the kitchen. Somehow she had figured out that I planned to leave.

After giving her a piece of apple, I went back into the bedroom to continue getting ready. I had barely zipped the suitcase shut when she was back up on the bed, looking more than just a little perturbed. Parrots, especially macaws, hate being fooled. It must go against some kind of bird code, and I had crossed a line.

"Aaack, aaack!" It wasn't a soft scream. This was a pissed-off parrot. She walked over to the closed case and climbed on top. Although it was not specially constructed to withstand macaws, the only obvious protuberances were the handle and the luggage tag that hung from it. I was fast; she was faster. I grabbed the bag; she grabbed the tag. Human 1, Bird 1. Now we were even.

Until I left, the suitcase sat in my car awaiting my departure, clothes wrinkling by the minute. My first day at the hotel would be a date with the ironing board.

The day to leave came, and I said my good-byes to all of my babies. Ben and Blanco knew the drill and walked into the bedroom to semi-hibernate until I returned. The cats were oblivious; enough food, and they were content. Kerry was preparing himself for whatever might occur; he had no idea what to expect but was confident that he and Lori could handle it, along with help from Samantha if needed.

"I love you, Sarah, but Mommy has to go on a trip. I'll be back, I promise." Her pupils were pinpricks and her head was down. She knew. As I turned to walk out the door, her words nearly stopped my trip before it started.

"Love you."

For all the times I had told her how much I loved her, that was the first time she had responded in kind. The walk to the car was one of the hardest of my life.

CHAPTER 16

When I returned from New York, Sarah's demeanor had changed. Her eyes seemed somehow darker and she followed me everywhere—not so much out of devotion, more out of desperation. The front door had taken me somewhere she couldn't go. She wanted out.

Ultimately, though, the ravens were the final straw. There were three mated pairs (they mate for life) and two unmated ravens who came to the first of three ponds to drink and bathe. Sarah could easily see them as they interacted with one another, foraged for food, and played in the water. In some rather perverse way, I think they must have teased her with their caws and calls because their arrival always created havoc in the house. Sarah would climb on top of her cage for a better view and create a total body fluff that made her look twice her size. Her pupils would narrow and her head would move up and down in dramatic thrusts, all the while as she was screaming at her black tormentors. They would respond by calling back to her with their "Awk, awk, awk" acknowledgments. Then, if Blanco were outside, the drama would shift to his chasing the ravens away from the pond and back up into the trees. By that time, the cacophony of macaw screams, terrier barks, and raven caws made telephone discussions impossible. Fortunately, I had by now explained to all of my publishers, editors, and clients that I had a macaw.

The ravens were the tipping point. I had to decide whether or not to let Sarah go outside. First, I went to Samantha, who had lost her favorite cockatoo in a free-flight situation. She had been, and still is, devastated over Jasmine's death. Her warning was clear: If you free-flight your bird, it's only a matter of when, not if, the bird will be lost or die. What to do? Sarah had begun life as a free bird. She had known the loft of wind in her feathers; she had soared over trees and rivers; she had been a careful Icarus guided by years of evolution and experience. Could the forest become her new jungle?

I set about doing research. I read, I interviewed, I analyzed. Opinions were divided. A physician who managed a flock of twenty free-flighted macaws had never had a problem. The birds nested in his oak trees year-round, including in rain and snow. They sometimes flew as far as the Mendocino coast, thirty miles away, but always returned. Then there was the Chicago-transplant engineer who had brought his macaw pair from the Windy City to the gentle firs of Ukiah, just twenty miles south of us. Not only did his macaws free-flight along with being in the house, where they nested, they had also free-flighted when they were in Chicago. They would fly all over the city in all kinds of weather and always knew how to find their way home. Who knew that the Sears Tower could be a homing device? I was being swayed. I decided that if Sarah could articulate her opinion, she would choose to take her chances with the world outside her door. The house, with all my best intentions and effort, had simply become a bigger cage—a cruel cage out of which she could see what she could not have. It had been one year since she had come to us. I knew what to give her for her birthday.

That day in May, my own birthday month, began calmly and like any other in Sarah's life. The dogs went outside, the cats went outside, and she watched as I moved toward the door to go outside. She was on her bamboo stand, which stood less than a foot from the door opening. She inclined her body forward. "Just maybe, just maybe . . ." I looked at her with an expression she must have understood, because she immediately straightened up her body and stared at me, pupils wide.

"Sarah, I have a surprise for you. You're going to be a free bird. Free, Sarah, the way you are supposed to be. Okay, are you ready to be a free bird?"

With that, I opened the door wide to its three-foot span. Then I stepped out onto the deck. Sarah hung as far forward on the bamboo screen as she could without actually falling off. She waited. Had I made a mistake? Had I somehow forgotten to close the door? Slowly she climbed down off the screen and stood at the door's opening. Then she stepped across the track, out onto the deck. First she looked down. She could see the ground below through the spaces between the boards. Then she looked around, not moving, as if a misstep would quickly find her back inside the house and behind the glass door. I walked to the edge of the deck and sat down. She walked over to me and looked down over the edge at the exposed ground. Now her pupils were pinpoints. I waited, tensed, for the sound of her wings as they whooshed her off the deck. The sound never came. Instead, she walked over to where the stairs made a four-step descent to the waiting garden. And stopped.

She would start slowly. She would start with the steps. There was no turning back.

CHAPTER 17

There from the edge of the deck she peered down into the space between the top of the deck and the first stair. Beneath the deck were dirt and weedy growth, along with a couple of abandoned dog toys. Abandoned not just by the dogs but by me as well; going into the crawl space under the house to reach them would have brushed me up against ancient spiderwebs and possibly a startled raccoon.

The dogs were off by one of the little ponds, oblivious to the activity on the deck. The cats were nowhere to be seen. Soon everyone would see the adventure unfolding. Sarah moved away from the stairs and decided to explore the deck itself first. Potted plants and baskets rimmed much of the deck; the baskets served as sleeping stations for several of our cats. None of them was very heavy; none of them was sturdy enough to withstand The Beak. I had expected her to first check out the plants—a little greenery as a snack, perhaps. But no, the baskets were far too tempting—and familiar from her forays into the dogs' toy basket inside. She poked at the first one, Tiger's favorite, but instead of crunching down she chose a different approach: tossing it over the edge of the deck. After it bounced into the petunias, she walked over to the edge of the deck in order to assess her beak toss. Apparently it wasn't up to her standards, because she immediately went to the next basket and launched it even higher. This time she reached the geraniums; next, the dahlias. Within fifteen minutes she had cleared the deck, literally, of all empty baskets. Tiger, who must have been anticipating a late-morning nap, returned to find his favorite basket upended in the petunias. From there, it was a short eye scan before he saw Sarah at the edge of the deck. He quickly scooted under the deck and under the house. Sarah stood tall, triumphant once again.

I, on the other hand, had not just stood there passively while she hurled. I carefully moved the potted plants (those I could lift) down to the easterly stairs, where they would be safe until she learned how to climb down. The largest plant, which I could not move, was a queen palm that I had brought from my previous home, where it was indeed the majestic queen of my little tropical garden. But there was a new queen in town.

Similar in some ways to jungle plants familiar to Sarah, the palm was a climbing invitation, and Sarah accepted. Unlike the dracaena next to the woodstove, the palm at first seemed sturdy and Sarah started her ascent with confidence. Halfway up, the palm revealed its lighter side and the bird found herself thrashing among the leaves for a way back out. She fell off onto the deck, and now she was a bird with a purpose.

RULE 6: IF YOU CAN'T CLIMB IT, EAT IT

Back up she climbed, now safely perched on the basket's edge. The lowest palm frond disappeared in one clean strafe, immediately followed by a second and third leaf. Given her height and beak speed, it would only take seconds to lose nearly half of the tree.

Time for the feather duster. Gently I coaxed Sarah to the other end of the deck, hoping that she would begin to explore the stairs as an opportunity to discover bigger territory. She stood on the edge as before, looking down to the ground below, but it wasn't time. She walked back into the house and climbed back up on her bamboo stand.

I left the door open and stepped down into the garden, retrieving the baskets and placing them back on the deck. She watched while I did so. When I knelt down to lift up the dahlia heads that had been torpedoed, she climbed back down and walked to the edge of the deck, right above my head. She leaned over and turned her head to one side. Then she laughed.

CHAPTER 18

WE BEGAN a new morning ritual: Let the dogs out, let the cats out, let Sarah out. Now, in addition to macaw mumblings, my business calls would be punctuated by the twitterings of wild birds and frogs in full chorus. I liked to think that I was bringing Zen moments to my concrete-bound editors.

It would take Sarah roughly a month to fully navigate the stairs. The first step was the hardest. She tried to bend over and catch the step's surface with her beak as a stabilizing point. She bent a little too far and then pulled back. Then she tried to reach the stair with her footed leg, but again it was too far. Then she executed a maneuver I wouldn't have expected. She turned around, her back to the stair below, bent over sideways to the deck, grabbed the wood with her beak, and flipped herself to the waiting stair. Her first landing was a bit rough and tumble, but by the time she pulled the same maneuver for the second and third steps, she almost bounced from one to the next. The last step was only three inches off the ground, and now she hopped off with confidence, real terra firma under her.

Looking a little like the proverbial deer in the headlights, she just stood there. She looked down; she looked up; she looked around. Her first step for birdkind was slow and deliberate, as if to be sure she was really on solid ground. Her next step was more of a tiny hop, and then she was hurtling full stride toward the redwood table only a few feet ahead.

Ah, a new perch. It was an easy climb, and now she was four feet off the ground and able to survey what had previously been only a view to a thrill. She fluffed her feathers and began to preen. She outstretched her wings so as to feel real air under them. She flapped but stayed on top of the table. This was not the jungles of South America; she needed to visually process what was familiar and what was new.

What were probably most different, and potentially most challenging, were the trees themselves. Our property is covered in firs, which can reach 100 feet; madrones, which can top nearly 80 feet and which have smooth, nearly unclimbable bark; tan oaks, which rarely reach 20 feet; and the occasional pine, which can reach 80 feet. The tallest trees are the firs, whose presence blocks light from the other trees, which grow shorter and thinner as a result. In some places the trees have created what is known as a climax forest, where thinner trees are only two or three feet apart. The only clear space, on the road side of the house, is actually an open circle surrounded by 80- to 100-foot firs. This was

Sarah's new flying space, far different from the jungle canopy she had flown above in her native home. For now, the redwood table gave her a perspective of up to about 20 feet. She would have to go higher to assess the bigger picture.

The bigger picture was a while in developing. For the first couple of months, Sarah was content with the redwood table or the surrounding garden floor. She quickly notched the table for easier climbing and marked the ground around the table with droppings. This "living fence" marked the boundaries of her new space. Other birds never approached when she was there, something that surprised me. Given how brightly colored she was, I would have thought their curiosity would have drawn them in. Even the ravens out by the first pond could clearly see her there, but they always kept to their own territory. Nor did she express interest in them once she was outside. How strange. While inside, she and the ravens were loud and raucous to each other. But here, with no barriers, some other instinct must have taken over. Species respect and distance, no doubt.

In the first few days of her new freedom, I confined my gardening to the central garden, which surrounded the redwood table. Roughly sixty by forty feet, this once barren patch was now laid out with raised flower beds, ornamental trees and shrubs, a bonsai corner, a cactus corner, and a "rust garden" created out of all the rusty collectibles that Kerry had salvaged in his contracting work. For months they had all just been dumped into a pile where my office cottage now stands. Looking much like the abandoned pile of bricks that I had transformed into the yellow brick road, the pieces had a purpose, which I chose to be a whimsical sculpture corner where plants and flowers in complementary colors played in and among the angles. When my garden was nominated for an award, it was the rust garden that people loved most. All of these areas were Sarah's new outdoor world. Within those first few days, Sarah decided it was time to climb down off her table and check out the fauna.

What was I thinking? Much as when I had accepted Sarah into my life, I did not think. I led with my heart. Looking back, would I rationally have chosen a bird who would destroy valuable furniture, chew whatever her beak fancied, shred important papers, terrorize our other animals, and threaten my health? Of course not. The gift of love is cleverly wrapped, and it is a wise fool who unties the package. Even today, when I walk down the deck stairs, my hand on the railing that Sarah eventually learned to master, I can feel the ridges and pits her beak created in order to navigate the steep angle. The clematis that became her stairway to heaven still shows the marks of her grasping. The redwood table, her first outdoor perch, has weathered the scratches she made with her singular claw. I am grateful for my naive choices, which allowed her such freedoms. Everything else is only particles and dust.

The garden was my sanctuary; the artful combination of color, scent, and configuration was a balm to the visual chaos inside the house. When I was in the garden, the trailer disappeared. When Sarah was in the garden, her cruel capture disappeared. Together we shared a paradise that no one else could touch. Even the dogs and cats kept their distance when she and I were outside. Not out of fear; respect.

Of course, there were the plants. At first Sarah seemed more interested in dirt. Perhaps because she had watched me digging in various flowers and bulbs, she saw dirt as "kindergarten." I had no idea that macaws were diggers; to this day, I'm not sure that this is a primal instinct, but for Sarah dirt was delight. It was bulb-planting season when Sarah first discovered dirt. I was carefully digging tiny holes, filling each with bulb starter, and then placing each bulb tenderly into its waiting home. In total, I planted nearly two hundred bulbs that first season with Sarah; she simply watched for the first twenty or so, standing right next to my hand as I "clawed" and cultivated. "Claw" refers here to the only garden tool I use, a four-pronged workhorse that does everything except dig deep holes. Somewhere around the twenty-first bulb, Sarah must have decided that this was an exercise well within bird bounds. Without prompting, she began to dig a small hole, using her beak like a trowel or "claw." When her hole looked like the one I had just dug, she stopped. She looked at me for what to do next. I was stunned. I decided to honor her work by sprinkling bulb starter in her new hole, along with the one I had just dug. She stood there, almost as if to say "Now's when you put the bulb in the hole." So I did. I then pushed the soil back into the hole, covering the newly planted bulb. Sarah pushed at the soil just a little, then looked at me to complete what she had started. I finished the hole and smiled. Satisfied, Sarah went on to other garden curiosities, obviously content that she was a useful bird. Every year when those bulbs bloom—tulips, crocus, lilies of the valley, narcissus, daffodils—I try to remember which little holes Sarah helped dig.

Dirt also meant bugs. From mealy bugs to earwigs to ants (including fire ants) to potato bugs to scorpions, the soil was home to all. I didn't then, nor do I now, wear gloves. I need to feel the dirt in my hands; my nails are testament to this passion. Four times a year when I go to New York, I must face the manicurist to restore my nails to some semblance of "professional." Those trips aside, my hands and nails are those of a gardener. Sarah loved dirt; she also loved bugs. The fire ants were in only one location, so I did no gardening there. Any plants in that area were in pots. I also avoided a second location where yellow jackets had a ground nest. I had discovered it only once, by accident, as I attempted to dig in a new plant, blithely unaware that a nest was only inches from my hands. When one wasp flew at me, I dismissed it like some benign mosquito. It was quickly followed by two or three more, and then, before I could react, the entire nest was at my face and upper body. I ran, faster than I still believe possible, in an effort to outrun the angry fliers. I was lucky, because I wear glasses, that they stung only the areas around my eyes and cheeks. I blocked my mouth with my arm, which took the brunt of the attack. After fifty feet or so, they retreated, and Sarah could see—and hear—my distress. It took almost a week for the swelling to go down, and in truth my husband "nuked" the nest to prevent any further attacks. Still, and to this day, I avoid that area just in case.

So the bugs Sarah engaged were not dangerous, with the exception of the occasional scorpion. In bulb-planting season scorpions are nearly hibernational and barely move when disturbed. In this mode they are easily dispatched. Normally I would simply flick or nudge the sleeping stinger to a place beyond my digging. Sarah, on the other hand, would "catch and release," quickly grabbing and then tossing the somnombulent creature into the air. Once the scorpion she tossed was already dead, and I was shocked to see her attempt a small feast. It must have been past its expiration date because she threw it aside after only one bite. She did fancy mealy bugs but not in quantity. Mostly, it was all about the dirt. Oh, yes, and the plants.

Thanks to the likes of Alice Waters, everyone knows that many flowers are edible. Certainly, none of the species in my garden grew in South America, but they must be distant cousins. Like a tourist at a Las Vegas buffet, Sarah grazed the flower beds in search of floral cuisine. Her favorites were geraniums and roses. The geraniums she ate slowly and deliberately, avian connoisseur that she was becoming. The roses were a different matter. These she playfully pulled apart, one petal at a time, munching one occasionally but mostly satisfied by the apparently universal game of "He loves me, he loves me not." Some people say that flowers have faces. If that is true, those faces were not smiling. But Sarah was, and the flowers would grow back.

CHAPTER 19

Freedom brought another change to our relationship. Now that she had some of the same access to house and garden as I did, her attitude underwent a transformational shift.

One of the amazing things about macaws, certainly Sarah, is that they have a profound sense of fair play and respect. As a bird "partner" or mate, you have to start your relationship by understanding that a macaw is a bird and birds behave as they have for thousands of years. They aren't little people who will go gently into the world of humans and become a "little person." I see the same expectation with so many human parents who become upset when their three-year-old becomes defiant, tests the limits of their environment, screams, becomes finicky about the food he or she eats, or gets feisty with his or her siblings. Big surprise—they're three! Macaws are perennially three years old, and Sarah was always testing the boundaries of our relationship. I was constantly assessing my reactions, responses, and remediation when necessary. Required above all was consistency, which moves right into fair play. If she was intrigued by the pages of a manuscript rife for the shredding, my response was always "No." Not always "No" at the beginning, however. Thinking she would be amused by shredding the pages of a magazine about to be recycled (and to distract her from something else), I failed to consider that for a bird paper is paper. When she then tried to escalate to a manuscript and I scolded her, she looked at me with indignation. I finally learned consistency after she destroyed a publishing contract that was lying next to me on the daybed as I talked on the phone. Sarah was behind me on the bamboo screen, and it took only seconds for her to jump down and grab the document in her beak. Paper doesn't do well with push and pull, and at least a third of the document was ripped beyond salvage. I was devastated. It's one thing for publishers to find my bird escapades amusing, quite another for me to have to request a new signature copy of a contract. Lesson learned, I now forbade any paper chewing and Sarah acquiesced, but only after weeks of "No paper, Sarah!"

Consistency definitely involved language. The first verbal test was food. Despite Sarah's varied diet, she always aspired to the food I ate. She didn't care what Kerry was consuming; I was her mate. Mostly, I ate meals on the daybed because the trailer had no dining table space. In warm weather I would often eat outside on the redwood table, where Sarah had no access to my food—that is, of course, until Sarah was allowed to go outside. Whichever place I dined, Sarah was becoming adamant about sharing my food. In the wild, macaws do share food with each other and eating is an intimate, communal activity; so why wouldn't Sarah want to share vittles with me? Being a "parent" like so many I know, I would sometimes give her a morsel, other times not. Bad idea. In bird parlance "sometimes" means "always." So I developed a two-word solution: "My food." Now when I ate, in addition to a knife and fork, I used the feather duster. Every time she attempted to purloin a taste, I would gently push her away or down from my plate. She was not a quick learner; it took days of saying "My food!" over and over again to the point where my interest in food sharply decreased. Finally she accepted the new rule. Each time she responded to my words, I would respond to her with "Thank you, Sarah; thank you for being a good bird." Then I would give her the last tiny morsel of my meal. She was being respected, and I was being fed.

Other words and expressions followed the same development pattern. "Bedtime" meant she had to go back up on her perch. Her personal inclination was to follow us into the bedroom and climb up on the foot of the bed. Yes, I was tempted; she looked so sweet sitting there with her sleepy eyes, just wanting to be close. And, yes, I did allow her to do so on one occasion. Result: during the night she climbed onto the bed and ended up sleeping next to me. Dangerous ground. If I moved suddenly or if Kerry happened to be feeling amorous, she might have reacted by attacking the source of her surprise. After that, it took more days of reiterating "Bedtime" until she accepted her perch as the place to sleep. There was also "Worky worky," a cutesy way of expressing that I was going into town, where my downtown office was located. When an owner leaves a bird's sight or auditory field, the bird has no way of knowing where its human is going or if he or she will ever return. Especially because Sarah had been so traumatized, I felt it was essential to telegraph my moves. Even before "Worky worky" I had used the word "Outside" when I was going into the garden; she learned that I was not far and did not become anxious over where I had gone. The agitation started after she had settled in and the weather had become warm. Still, she knew that I wasn't abandoning her. The same held true for when I went into Willits; she quickly learned that I would return in a matter of hours. During my absence she made no forays into mischief; when I got home, she would be on her perch, sentinel in my absence.

"Trip" was the hated word, especially after my recent New York adventure. Only once, when I was gone just overnight, was there a problem. That night, she flew off her perch at night, most likely in search of me in the bedroom, and crashed onto the daybed, scaring herself mightily. Macaws have virtually no night vision and are helpless in the dark. She also began to scream, and Kerry was quickly learning what it was like to live with an unhappy bird. The next day, I came home to a totally pissed-off parrot. Not since we had first gotten her had she tried to bite me. Now I needed to be punished for abandoning her without notice. I had given her notice but had used the wrong words. The next week was all about making nice and restoring our relationship. She did nip me a couple of times, drawing blood, but nothing that some Betadyne and a Band-Aid couldn't fix.

Consistency was the key. With consistency in both language and actions, respect grew. With respect came a stronger relationship for us and less antagonism for the other animals. If I offered a treat to one, I offered a treat to all and always in the same order. Sarah was given her treat first; then she waited for the dogs to be given theirs before the treat cycle was repeated. I was actually behaving like a good parent. I was pleased.

After almost a year, my consistency was paying off. The animals were more settled, and Kerry could feel a better sense of order in the house. But as I have learned about the ways of a macaw, things can change without warning. If she gave me such a warning, I missed it.

CHAPTER 20

SARAH'S NEW FREEDOM impinged on the freedom of all the other animals, who had adapted quickly to a caged bird but who had become severely compromised by her cage-free life. I was the well-meaning villain who had now exposed them to all manner of assaults. My business was also becoming severely compromised by her unpredictable behavior.

For the dogs it meant scattered food, bathing water to drink, dismembered toys, and physical attacks. There was also a decline in their intimate time with me. Hugs and pets had to be out of Sarah's presence or she would interrupt our affections. Though she was willing to tolerate the others, she would not share me with them. For a short time after the outside world was opened up to her, their outdoor escapades were unaffected by her small forays into the flower beds and sandbox. They would play elsewhere, and all of us could have been subjects in Edward Hicks's painting "The Peaceable Kingdom." Digging was the key to the next canine affront. As Sarah's digging territory expanded, she found a new place whose only greenery was clover in uneven patches. Rhythmically she began troweling the dirt with her beak, unearthing the occasional bug and content with shallow holes. Then she struck something hard, something off-white that smelled vaguely (I presume) like old meat. Bones. Not just one bone buried haphazardly, but Blanco's bone collection, which had a time stamp of at least two or three years.

Blanco was neurotic; when I gave him and Ben each a bone, Ben would immediately lie down and begin to gnaw on his gift. Blanco, on the other hand, afraid perhaps that it might be the last bone he ever got, would grab his treasure and look for a place to bury it. I never followed him, so I had no idea where his buried treasure was located. Sarah had struck pay dirt. True to her original name bestowed mockingly by her captors, Peg Leg was about to demonstrate how much of a pirate she was. She rolled the first small bone, probably a pork rib, around in her beak like a connoisseur. Apparently it failed the test, because she dug her beak back into the dirt in search of better specimens. The bone toss had started. Chicken, lamb, pork, beef all became a juggling act while Sarah loudly chortled at her prowess. Not unlike the ape in *2001: A Space Odyssey* when it discovers the power of bones, Sarah could not have looked more primeval. Between chortles she would raise her wings and extend them full width, bobbing her head up and down in victory. Blanco watched in horror from the deck. I think it was horror, but maybe it was more like doom.

Sensing his anguish, I went back into the house and retrieved a piece of steak—no bone—to offer him in his pain. His eyes brightened and he gulped the steak, comforted in the knowledge that Sarah had no access to his treat in its present location. Of course, that gesture created a new demand on his part, just to keep things fair. No longer was he interested in bones; why bother? From now on it had to be meat, and I, like the guilt-ridden mother of all times, continued to feed his pain.

I had taken to placating the cats as well. Since their comings and goings into and out of the house now required ninja talent, I felt they needed to be compensated for the occasional tail nip or flight off the daybed, so I added fresh fish to their diet. Sarah had no nose (beak, really) for fish, and she never attempted to snatch their sole. It was a little more redemption for me. With Kerry, the biggest sacrifice for him was in the bedroom. We had always had a passionate sex life. Until Sarah.

The occasions of our lovemaking were varied; mornings were our usual favorite. On weekends, the daybed offered spur-of-the-moment "afternoon delight," with an occasional foray into the outdoors. Having no visible neighbors is a real benefit of living in the woods. Once Sarah had decided that *she* was my mate, Kerry and I exchanged spontaneous for furtive. Nights were safe only after we had turned off all the lights. Mornings had become compromised by the presence of an audience. The dogs had never been watchers, and I'm convinced the cats thought we were behaving without decorum; they should talk. But here we would be, amorous and cuddly, when we would hear the patter of one foot as she approached the bedroom. Up she would climb and there she would sit, watching—intently, I might add—while we attempted some degree of pleasurable activity. At various points she would turn her head sideways, as if to better appraise whether or not we were adept. Other times she would bob her head up and down, and we felt as if we were being given two thumbs up. At other times, always the wrong times, she would laugh loudly, and there we were at coitus interruptus. We ultimately became night lovers, like two teenagers keeping quiet in a parent's house. Sarah, on the other hand, slept soundly on her perch, choosing acceptance to animosity.

Then there was me as a businesswoman. In order to conduct business in the house, I had to modify everything, in particular how my desk was set up (Kerry had built a corner desk for himself into a corner of the kitchen that overlooked the forest and had two big windows for light). If I chose to work there, I had nearly ten feet of surface space to accommodate my papers. Underneath the desk were file drawers and storage so that everything on the surface was orderly. For me, order as well as aesthetics is essential; creativity and efficiency are impossible in chaos. My husband, on the other hand, thrives in chaos, and our first two years together were a challenge beyond words. Then along came Sarah.

Once she discovered indoor flight and the butcher block landing pad, it was a puddle jump to the kitchen corner desk. What to do? There had to be a barrier, and it couldn't be climbable. It also couldn't be solid because that would rob the kitchen—already a dismal affair—of its much-needed light. My solution belongs right in there with some of the greatest home improvement solutions ever discovered. As I have seen done in small New York apartments that require separation between areas in the same room, I chose a ceiling-mounted rod with a beautiful ecru fabric, nearly translucent, that could be hung on rings. I chose rings because the fabric could be hung lower from the rod and thus let in more light, while not allowing enough fly space for Sarah. The fabric was weighted at the bottom so as to hang better, and I bought a long length that caused it to drape on the floor by nearly a foot. After it was installed I prayed I had been correct in my thinking. Sarah had been watching from the butcher block, turning her head from side to side, trying to figure out what we could possibly be doing. When the job was completed, we walked back into the kitchen to see what Sarah would do. She climbed down off the stand (she had methodically notched the legs in case she wanted to climb, not fly) and cautiously walked over to "the wall." She pushed her head against it in several places and pulled at some of the fabric. Because the floor drape was long, she couldn't lift it high enough to crawl under; and when she tried to push through, she only succeeded in covering herself in fabric and she backed away. Could it be? Had I really achieved a total bird victory? Yes. I hugged Kerry and walked into a safe little corner of the world. Serenity.

Serenity did not include the screams. Even if I were twenty feet away, Sarah's screams were earsplitting. They were also especially well timed. When she got all the attention she wanted, she was fine. When my attention turned to publishers and authors, she resented the intrusion and did all in her power to regain that attention. At times I moved all over the house in search of quiet, including the bathroom, where I would close the door. Sarah would "knock" on the door, and eventually the screams would continue. Only when I allowed her outside did the screaming subside. She must have decided it was a fair trade for her freedom.

Having friends over was another new challenge. It's one thing if a bird is in a cage; people "ooh" and "aah," all the while safe from talons and beak. With Sarah out of her cage our friends fell into one of two camps: those who weren't afraid of birds and those who were. For the latter, we entertained outdoors or at their homes. For the former, it was interesting for them to discover that Sarah couldn't have cared less if they were there. She never attacked; she didn't scream. She simply sat upon her cage perch and watched. Perhaps she was taking mental notes. I had already made mine: Chaos is just a step on the way to order and serenity. "Soon, when all of these people leave, I will be the one here. I am the one." And she was.

CHAPTER 21

THE MORE COMFORTABLE Sarah became in one environment, the more she sought out new challenges. Just when I thought one environment had reached a point of predictability, she would surprise me again.

It had now been several weeks since Sarah's world had been expanded to include the great outdoors, and our rituals stayed focused on the ground. She had lost most of her interest in the redwood table and was for all intents and purposes a walking bird. Much as I would have loved to see her fly and recapture some of her wildness, I did feel much safer with her foot on the ground. She had become my little dog, following me wherever I went, happy just to share my company. With language, she was not inclined to learn more than a few words: "Thank you," "Welcome" for "You're welcome," "Love you." In addition, she had abandoned the early hippie-speak she had brought into our relationship. Most macaws are not compulsive talkers like African greys or other parrots. With macaws, actions do indeed speak louder than words; they are the enterprising mechanics of the bird universe. In her own way she was a professor of physics implementing various universal laws and testing their application. Outdoors, the challenges were less complex than they were inside.

In the kitchen, the cabinet under the butcher block had been secured with flip-down latches that could not be broken or pulled loose. The bears had already tried and failed. Sarah tugged and tongued without success, until she made a remarkable discovery. If she lifted the latch up and then down, it released.

She climbed down and into the cabinet. She had never encountered a can, so the first order was to check it out with her tongue. She tested the rim, the surface, the sides. She tried to pick one up by the rim, but it was too heavy and the rim was too small. At least that was true the first time she tried. Instead, she knocked one over. It rolled out of the cabinet, onto the floor. Power! Within a few minutes she had rolled all of the cans out of the cabinet. Now what? She hopped out of the cabinet and began to work her way among the cans, rolling them around the floor as she did so. By chance—or at least I think it was chance—she managed to grasp one of the smaller cans by the rim, and there it was: the outdoor bone toss all over again. Sarah tossed thirty cans all over the kitchen before deciding it was time for the great outdoors once again.

Out on the deck, I expected her to flip herself down the stairs as she always did. Not this time. Feeling especially inventive, she instead climbed one of the deck posts. That she had done before; she would then climb down and proceed to step flipping. This time she stayed on the post, looking down at the steeply sloped deck rail, which ended in another newel post at ground level. With her back to the rail, she descended the post until her foot reached the rail. Using her claw and leg for balance, she used her beak in a sideways grasp to climb down backward to the ground-connecting post. Once there, she climbed up the post, sat upon the newel, and surveyed her new perspective on the garden. For nearly twenty minutes she just sat there, looking especially beautiful as the sun caught the iridescent hues in her feathers. Eventually she climbed down to the ground. When her gardening was done, she climbed back up the post and this time pulled herself up the railing until she reached the deck. After that, stairs were a thing of the past. With months of ascending and descending, the rail became pitted and grooved, customized to her every move.

Only a few feet from the redwood table was a small madrone no more than six feet tall. The lower bark was still shaggy—thus climbable—and there were a few tiny branches that created a ladder effect. The top two feet were much smoother and less climbable, and its only extensions were twiglets. Sarah looked up, then down. I don't know if she was looking at the ground or at her one foot. Either way, this climb would be a challenge and take her higher than she had ever been before in the garden.

Surprisingly, the climb up was almost effortless. Perched on the top branch, she looked even more beautifully regal than she had on the newel post. For the first time, I saw her as a real, free bird—no cage perches, no deck railing or post, no butcher block, no bamboo screen. She was on a tree. Even from a height of six feet she could fly. Would she? Part of me wanted nothing more. Another part was terrified. This could be that moment of truth. What if she flew up instead of down? What if she flew too high to be recaptured? And how could I, or anyone else for that matter, recapture her? She couldn't be touched. Would she be able to climb down on her own? Could she fall, given her missing foot and claw? Or would she somehow fly out of my life forever, reclaimed by the sky?

I held my breath as she raised her wings and hunched her body. She made several false launch moves; my breath held with each one. Finally, she lofted briefly, changed her mind, and stepped down instead on one of the tiny twiglets nearest her foot. Too brittle to support her weight, it snapped and she flopped to the ground. Disappointment for her, relief for me, but not for long. Parrots are little bulldogs; they never give up. Back up the tree she went; this time, her movements were different. This was not about climbing; this was about flying. Once on the top branch, she wasted no time in getting into launch position, and then she did. Her first flight took her over the redwood table and on to another short tree with thicker branches. The first landing was awkward, but she didn't fall.

She stayed there for the rest of the afternoon. She bore a smile, a Buddha-like smile. She was finally home. It may not have been the home of dense jungles and fragrant flowers, but it was green, it was solid, and it smelled of the freedom so long denied her.

CHAPTER 22

THE SECOND TIME Sarah flew, it was from the same little tree she had landed upon when she took flight from the premier madrone. There in the curve of much taller firs she established her throne, and for a number of weeks this was her new outdoor home. She brandished a twig like a scepter. The garden floor no longer held interest for her, and the boneyard was returned to Blanco, though he never did reacquire his taste for bones.

The one-tree honeymoon didn't last as long as I had hoped. So many trees, so little time. Just before my birthday in May, when the fragrances of the late-spring flowers are intoxicating, the jasmine and clematis released their siren song. In my continuing efforts to cover the trailer with shrubs and flowers, I had planted waves of jasmine, three types of clematis, and climbing Banks roses. The roses were somewhat straggly; too many trees blocked the midday sun. But the jasmine and clematis thrived, climbing the trailer walls to the roof, where new growth cascaded back down over the walls, creating a fairyland of purple and white blossoms. The sight and smell were an invitation Sarah could not ignore. Hers was not a direct flight. That took a few more weeks of several new trees, each new perch slightly higher than the previous. At this time in May, her flight circle was roughly sixty feet and reached nearly fifteen feet high. She would fly from one stop to the next, visiting each tree like an old friend, at the same time gaining a much bigger view of her world. From fifteen feet she could even see the dark forest, but she never tried to fly there. Instead, she turned her attention to the trailer walls and began to search for a way to the roof.

She returned to the garden floor on a mission. No more digging holes or looking for aged bones. How could she make her way to the roof, which would afford her a grand vista above those smaller trees? The rose trellis. A thin, brittle redwood lattice, the trellis went from the ground to the roofline. One lattice square at a time, she ascended the precarious perch. Occasionally, a piece of lattice would splinter or break. Undaunted, she would find a new foothold, and the trek continued like this for hours. In a few hours she made it to the roofline, and I held my breath. From the roof serious flight was a real possibility, not only toward the dark forest but also to the open canyon just beyond our property line on the roadside. True, she would have to traverse hundred-foot firs to get there, but it was possible.

I looked up with a sense of both awe and dread. She spread her wings to their full width. It was clear; this was now her new home, and everything else was only a stairway to heaven. She had chosen her fate, and I accepted her decision. Her new world was good, and she rested. I had delivered on my promise.

Sarah also delivered on hers. When I called her to come back inside, she did. Carefully, she would climb down off the roof and over to the deck, climb her first post, tackle the railing, arrive at the second post, climb down, and walk across the threshold of her beginnings. She was the consummate barking parrot, walking bird, and flier. She was Icarus reclaimed.

CHAPTER 23

IT WAS SHORTLY after Sarah's first freedom flight that she became the barking parrot. Up until then, Blanco had owned the barking arena. Fearless in action (except with Sarah), he was fanatical with his voice. No one, no thing got anywhere near our property unannounced. His "intruder" bark was far more aggressive than his "announcement" bark. Then of course there was the "spider" bark, so named because any unexpected tiny movement or sound would bring about that very annoying rat terrier bark that pierces one eardrum and moves through your head to the other side. Maybe he was a spirit dog, one of those shamanic animals who works with "sighted" people. Whatever the reason, he was the great watchdog of all times.

Ben, on the other hand, was more of a "backup barker," like

the doo-wop singers standing behind a Motown group. Ben never barked first; he waited for Blanco to start, and then he would follow with a low resonance "woof." Not several woofs, just one. I guess he wouldn't have made a very good backup singer after all. So there was the barking duet, Blanco on lead microphone. Thus far, it was the only status mark he had in competition with the bird.

I managed to get Sarah to return inside from the garden by clapping my hands and acting "excited" to go back indoors. As a walking bird, she would respond immediately to my changing direction or moving to go back inside. After her inaugural flight, I was a little concerned that her newfound flight experience might be problematic in getting her to return to "dog obedience." While in the tree, she did watch me carefully as I moved about the garden. I purposely stayed in her line of vision so as not to precipitate a reactive launch, which might have taken her in a dangerous direction. From her current perch she had a 180-degree view of the garden toward the circle of sun nearest the road. Her view to the other 180 degrees was blocked by several large firs, which formed a rather tight semicircle and blocked her view of the denser woods beyond. Those woods were thick with trees nearly a hundred feet tall and in many places there were only several feet between them. That was my dark forest, the one place on our property that might prove Sarah's undoing. But here on her first tree, all around her was light forest with open spaces and numerous climbable trees to test her wings.

When afternoon light began to give way to dusk, I decided it was time to go back inside. I walked over to her tree and told her

I was "going inside," a term she had always responded to by getting right behind my feet and following me up the stairs.

"Inside, Sarah, inside. Mommy's going inside. Come on, Sarah, come on. Good girl!" With "Good girl!" she would always be right behind me, ready to return to her interior world. Would flight change her fealty?

As I moved away from her tree, she hunched and raised her wings, ready to fly again. "Please," I thought, "please climb down." She started to loft and then stopped. She looked up, she looked down, and then she flew—down. The landing was a bit rough, not as bad as her first flop landing but a little like a duck coming to rest on uneven terrain. Unperturbed, she fell into step and followed me to the stairs. Stairs? I don't think so. She was no longer in elementary school; stairs were for babies. She could climb; she could fly. Up the newel post she went, back up the rail, onto the top post, and back down to the deck floor. On her entrance back into the house she was a little taller, slightly more proud. This time when she climbed up to her cage perch, I did not see her as a caged bird with house privileges and limited garden access. She was a macaw. She was a winged beauty who could soar above my head and choose whatever perch she desired. She was now *ararar,* the Peruvian Indian name for parrot.

Back in the house, Blanco and Ben were enjoying the relative quiet of a house to themselves—no bird, no cats, no me. There was no way they could have known about Sarah's transformation. Blanco in particular could not have known that his barking status was about to be challenged. All parrots are excellent imitators of sound and language, if they choose. Sarah chose. Why after her first flight and not before? I have no way of knowing.

What I suspect is that her sense of self-esteem, so degraded by her previous life in captivity, had been restored and she was now ready to spread her "other wings" and show the world what she was made of.

I had gone into the bedroom to retrieve an extra pillow for the daybed when I heard the insistent barking. Looking out the window I saw nothing, but thinking that, spiders aside, Blanco was warning of some intrusion, I came back to the living room to see Blanco looking up at Sarah's cage perch. He no longer barked at her, something he had done to distraction for the first several weeks of her arrival. Perhaps there was something outside, so I opened the door and exhorted Blanco with my usual battle salvo, "Go, Blanco. Go get 'em, Blanco!" He really was a great protector, and I didn't want him to lose his edge.

Dutifully, so as not to damage his reputation, I'm sure, he took off like a rocket toward the dense forest, barking his advance as he ran. I saw nothing but stood patiently at the door. The bark startled me. The sound wasn't coming from the forest beyond; it was coming from above my head. In perfect pitch, Sarah was re-creating Blanco's staccato snipes and looking quite pleased with herself. Outside, Blanco heard the "barks" and frantically searched for the source of his competition. There he was, poor little guy, running hither and yon in search of the phantom barker. I, on the other hand, was stifling laughter that might have insulted Sarah. Before I succumbed to explosive guffaws, Sarah provided the punchline: "Heh, heh, heh." Bird 1; Dog −1.

From that point on I never knew which one to believe, the dog or the parrot. Was that really the UPS delivery truck or just Sarah developing her dog side? Was it only Sarah, or was there really a bear on the back porch? When the same neighbor who had introduced me to the local sheriff's department asked if there was a problem with Blanco because his barking had intensified, I took the same position I had assumed when the sheriff asked me if everything was all right: "Everything's fine."

CHAPTER 24

Sarah's canine shift continued with a silly little game called "Where's the Ben dog?" For reasons I still don't understand, dogs love to hide under a blanket or similar covering and pretend they're invisible.

It all started when I adopted Ben. I was sorting through old linens and towels for the "donate" basket when I noticed that Ben had disappeared. One minute he was on the floor watching me toss assorted blankets, sheets, tablecloths, and towels toward the oversize laundry basket; next thing I knew, he was nowhere to be seen.

"Ben dog; where are you, Ben dog?" That's how it started, with him under a blanket that had missed the basket.

"Woof, woof." His wiggly body gave him away, and I playfully poked at him with my fingers, all the while asking "Where's the Ben dog? Where's the Ben dog?"

Sarah had watched me do this numerous times. When Blanco joined our family, he became my surrogate. I would toss a blanket or towel over Ben, and Blanco would proceed to bite at him from on top of the covering. Then we'd switch, Blanco under cover and Ben trying to find him from on top. The barking parrot was onto her next canine merit badge.

No sooner had I retrieved the blanket from Ben and Blanco than Sarah hotfooted it over to the place on the floor where they had been. She grabbed a corner of the blanket and tried to pull it away from me.

"Sarah, do you want to play? Do you want to play 'Where's Sarah?' "

She tossed her corner of the blanket up and down, making sweet little ululations as she did so. This was strange. It was one thing for her to play in and around the laundry, but could she possibly want me to actually cover her up? In the capture and transportation of wild birds, they are covered and restrained in a number of ways. "Toweling" is the easiest way to immobilize a struggling bird, and most certainly she had been toweled more than once. The towel is thrown around the bird and then gathered in a quick twist and secured; the bird can then be moved without injury to the handler. What would she do if I threw the towel over her head? What to do, what to do?

Her head bobbing continued, and I decided to take it as a positive cue.

"Okay, Sarah. Let's play 'Where's Sarah?' "

Gingerly, I tossed the towel over her head and body, quickly pulling back my hand after I did so. Just in case.

"Heh, heh, heh!!! Heh, heh, heh!!!"

She loved it. Covered in fluffy cotton, she looked like a Halloween faux ghost playing beneath his or her sheet. How wonderful to see her embracing more of her canine side!

"Good girl, Sarah; good girl!"

Now the big test. Could I poke at her as I did with the dogs? That was their favorite part of the game. Was she ready for dog play?

"Okay, Sarah; here I come." I lightly poked at where her head was, hoping my fingers were faster than her beak if she decided to bite. No bite. Instead, she pushed the top of her head against my hand, laughing as she did so.

"Heh, heh, heh!"

Our little game went on for several minutes until she climbed out from underneath the towel, fluffed her feathers, and climbed back on top of her cage. The dogs had been watching in a state of disbelief while she tried to outdog them. Disgusted, they finally walked off, giving me a sidelong glance that spoke volumes.

I tried to reassure them: "Good boys, babies; good boys." My words paled in comparison to the look on Sarah's face.

Dogs 1, Bird 2.

CHAPTER 25

FINALLY Samantha was coming to visit. Sarah had been with us just under a year, and I was excited for Sam to see how wonderfully Sarah was doing. Samantha was proud, too, that her instincts about Sarah had been borne out by the experience I was enjoying with her.

"Hi, Nance, I'm so sorry it's taken so long to come up and see you. When Dr. Joel saw Sarah in your initial visit with him, he said how healthy she looked and how it just goes to show what love can accomplish."

Samantha walked over to Sarah's cage perch and looked up at the bird she had rescued. "Hi, Sarah; hi, baby. Oh, you look so beautiful up there."

Sarah performed her best head-to-the-side roll and then raised her wings in acknowledgment of what she heard.

"Nance, she looks great! Her feathers aren't oily, her eyes are bright, and her demeanor is back to 'macaw' pride."

I felt like a good mother who had saved her child from some tragedy. I *was* a good mother; I felt it, and now Samantha was confirming it.

"So what are you feeding her?" Good mother, going down.

Backing away slightly from the cage, Samantha looked down into one of the two food dishes. In the first was the organic bird kibble recommended by both Samantha and Dr. Joel, along with a variety of nuts—two each of almonds, walnuts, pistachios, and peanuts. This was Sarah's afternoon/dinner meal; in the morning, I gave her only one peanut as a good-morning gesture.

"Oooh, nuts! You have to be careful with those. If she eats too many, it will upset her digestive system. And seeds? You have to be careful with those, too. I see there aren't any sunflower seeds. Good; they're the worst."

Wait until she looks in the fresh produce dish.

Before I could respond with a seed/nut defense, she was poking into the fruits and vegetables. Sarah looked amused, as if she were enjoying my chastisement. What she didn't understand was that this woman was threatening her birdie buffet, which she loved.

"Celery is good, and the carrots, but you have to be careful with cucumbers and any veggie with seeds." Ah, seeds again. This time I was quick to respond.

"Actually, she spits them all over the floor; she never eats them." There, a partial defense.

"Pasta? Is that pasta—and meat?" The defense was slipping.

"You really shouldn't feed her human food; their stomachs just can't handle it." Thank God the chicken bone had already been dispatched.

"And you really should stay away from too much citrus; even bananas can be too rich for her. Wait, is that a cherry? Oh, never cherries!" From seeds to pits, which was where this conversation seemed headed.

"Samantha, she loves cherries, and she very carefully eats around the pit, then tosses it on the floor along with the seeds." Sarah looked as if she were keeping score, tilting her head from one side to the other as the two humans debated her culinary future.

"Well, it's up to you, of course, but I keep my birds on a very regimented diet and treats are only occasional."

"I really am careful, Samantha, and I talk to many other macaw owners to get input as well."

"That's good; perspective is so important."

With that we were on to more personal stories about bird antics and behavior, which brought us all too soon to the question of free-flighting.

"I've done a lot of research, including those two macaw owners in the valley who let their birds fly free. Sam, I've been letting Sarah go outside. She's so happy out there; I can't tell you what a joy it is to see her as a free bird." Dead silence, quickly followed by a solemn warning.

"Nance, you remember what happened to Jasmine? If you let her fly, it's not a matter of if but when." Tears welled up in her eyes, and I knew it was best to simply accept and acknowledge her concerns.

"I know, Sam, I know. It's just that she began her life as a free bird, and it genuinely hurt me to watch her confined in this 'cage' of a house. I truly believe I made the right decision."

The subject was dropped, and we moved into nonbird discussions before she had to return to her flock. After she left, I stood and looked at Sarah, who was now merrily cruising her buffet. With her beak half buried in "good food," she stopped to give me what looked like a side wink.

"Good girl, Nancy, good girl."

CHAPTER 26

THE EXPERIENCE with Samantha had left me feeling hollow. If Sarah was happy and healthy, didn't that mean that I was doing things the right way, the best way for both Sarah and me? Kerry tried to comfort me by saying that maybe Samantha was jealous of the relationship I had with Sarah and the fact that I had accomplished it in such a short time. No, I didn't think she was a jealous type of person. Still, I wasn't very comforted by his words; insecurities were creeping in. I needed to go visit Sam at her bird sanctuary and understand her multiple bird relationships better.

The bird rescue facility, which is also a wild mustang preserve, sits on a beautiful stretch of land with several outbuildings and a spacious main house. The most memorable image of my first visit was that of standing on the deck, macaws and cockatoos all around me and a small group of wild horses grazing not thirty feet away. "I could live here," I thought, content with my extended animal family.

"Hi, Nance, I'm so glad you came up here. After I left, I felt like I was pretty hard on you. I hope you didn't think I was being rude. It's just that I've raised and rescued so many birds, and sometimes too much love isn't the best thing for the bird."

"No, I wasn't upset; I just thought that I might need a better understanding of what's really best for Sarah—and for me, and for Kerry."

With that she led me to the first cage and the oldest of her macaws.

Tika was a blue-and-gold macaw, very old—although no one knew exactly how old—and unusually mellow. Her white cage was the size of Sarah's and boasted numerous toys for her amusement. The food dishes held exactly what Samantha advocated: kibble, no nuts, couscous, and green vegetables, including lettuce.

"Lettuce, really? I've tried that a couple of times, even experimenting with Bibb lettuces and the bitter ones. She throws them all on the floor."

"Macaws are fussy and have very different tastes from one bird to the next. Even Tika will love something one day and then drop it to the bottom of her cage the next."

"Same with Sarah. With her, food is a game of chance."

In the next cage was an umbrella cockatoo with its lemony head plume, a contrast to its milk white body, up to full height. The bird was truly splendid.

"That's Little Bit. His previous owner named him, and he seems to like it. He talks to himself all the time: 'Hi, Little Bit. Hello, big bird.' "

"Do you keep the names they're given, or do you choose new ones?" It was one of those questions a person asks for which the answer constitutes small talk. While I was peering into the food dishes, all of which were similarly stocked, Samantha was narrating a miniseries of bird stories—in total, she had thirty-nine birds since her new acquisitions. The image of black and white cages lined up around the three living room walls, each housing a colorful macaw, cockatoo, African grey, or small parrot, was almost dizzying. Mostly, the birds were quiet; but as soon as Samantha walked to Tika's cage to let her out, the music started.

"Aaack, aaack, aaack!" A variety of bird voices quickly became a din that only got worse when she then released the cockatoo as well.

"You get used to it."

"That's true. At first, Sarah's screams almost made me jump out of my skin; but now that I've let her go outside, she doesn't scream that much at all." Ooops, I'd stepped into the "outside" zone. This time, Samantha just flew over it and continued with her bird stories. All of these birds were rescue animals, most had lived in multiple homes, some had been physically abused, none had been free-flighted, and all were grateful to have a home that would always be there for them. I say "grateful" because it showed on their faces and in their posture. These were happy birds, even with their restrictive diets. They were healthy and nonaggressive, even though some of them had been biters when they arrived. Mark and Samantha had loved them into gentle submission.

"Twice a day, Mark and I let out one or two of the birds that are safe to release for at least twenty minutes. If a bird doesn't want to come out, that's fine, too."

It was obvious to me that these birds had reasonable freedom; the window moldings were chewed, the furniture was scarred, and the slate floor was in constant need of being cleaned.

"Don't they ever fight with each other when they're out?"

"Oh, sure. Every once in a while a tiff breaks out, but it's rarely serious. Just in case, I always have a towel ready to grab the aggressor, along with plenty of styptic powder to stop the bleeding."

Better add that to my "good mother" list.

With that, we headed out to the aviary to see the macaws, who lived outdoors year round. The structure was the size of our trailer, only wider, and roughly fifteen feet high. There was a small "house" with two small doors, inside which were various perches and nesting boxes. The outdoor portion of the aviary was festooned with climbing apparatus and thick branches. Out here, they could fly. How lovely.

"What happens in the winter when it snows?" I couldn't imagine tropical birds in snowsuits.

"Mostly, they stay outside. Macaws are the toughest of the parrots when it comes to climate variables."

I tried to imagine Sarah in the snow, leaving one-footed prints as she toured our winter garden. That would be a sight to behold. Samantha and I bantered a little more, and then I noticed something I'd never seen before.

"Sam, why does that blue-and-gold have a band around his ankle?"

"It signifies they're wild-caught; it's put on right after they're captured, before they're sent to the United States. You can have a vet take it off, but it's not easy and you run the risk of hurting the bird's foot. They don't seem to mind, so we just leave them on."

I wondered where that blue-and-gold had come from. Had he flown the same jungle as Sarah? When he slept, did he dream of the Amazon?

"Well, I'm glad he found you. At least here he can fly." I was feeling better about the differences in style between Samantha and me. Comparison, say Chinese philosophers, is the source of all unhappiness. I didn't need to compare myself to the bird maven.

"Samantha, thank you so much for having me come up here. You've really been helpful and supportive, and I can't thank you enough for Sarah. She's going to have a very good life with me and Kerry."

"I knew you'd be the perfect mother for her, and you are."

CHAPTER 27

OUR HOUSEHOLD was full of adventure but not chaotic in the big picture. Sarah had finally settled in with all the other animals and they with her; Kerry was amazed at how so many could live so well together in such a small space. I was feeling like a very good mother. Therein lies my curse. Enter Big Bird and Ernie.

Big Bird and Ernie were two wild-caught, cherry-headed conures. Both had been banded with a metal circlet around one ankle. Transported from Central or South America, they had endured a terrible journey. Caught mostly in parrot snares or nets, the birds are quickly grabbed and two pieces of cardboard are wrapped around their wings, secured with a large rubber band. They are then tossed into a crate and dispatched to strange new worlds. The mortality rate is high; only the toughest birds survive, only to find themselves placed in a cage for the rest of their lives. Their life span can easily be forty years or more, so the confinement is a long one. Like macaws' over the past ten to fifteen years, their life span is shrinking while the number of homes for each "pet" bird increases. Such parrot capture is illegal today; however, the trade continues, with a recent estimate putting the number of captive parrots in America at 20 million, with some estimates pointing to as many as 40 million if one includes the parrots kept by breeders.

When I first saw Big Bird and Ernie, they were in a smallish cage at our local pet store. It was an innocent trip on my part, just going to replenish food for all of our various animals. By now, maybe, I should know better.

"Hi, Nance, I see you can't help but notice the two little guys." Beryl is the owner of the store, and she knows every animal lover's weakness. For me, it had become wild things in cages, and here they were. My husband was on a two-week motorcycle trip and there was no way to reach him for a discussion. Dare I even consider what I was considering?

"Okay, Beryl, give me the story. What are these guys doing here?"

"Their third owner got fed up with not being able to touch them, and his wife got fed up with cleaning their cage. They're about eight years old, and they're wild-caught."

At least they both have two feet, I thought to myself. They were absolutely adorable and looked very sad. Pressed up against each other, they looked out at me, their eyes empty of light. I couldn't bear it.

"How much?" My question really didn't need an answer, because whatever they cost, they were going home with me. I would consider their cost my "motorcycle trip," not that Kerry begrudged me anything. Still, he was going to be surprised when he got home. Ah, home. Where exactly was I going to put their cage in our already overcrowded living room? I'd figure something out. One thing about living in a small space, you become the doyenne of six inches.

"Four hundred fifty dollars, including the cage. I think you can even fit the cage in your car."

The car. When I had arrived at "Bell Acres," my cherished car was a 1962 Mercedes 190 SL with two tops, rag and metal. Midnight blue with red leather upholstery and a genuine ivory steering wheel (gulp!). I loved that car not because of any status attached to such a vintage automobile but because it was truly beautiful and because it transformed the driving experience. I kept it spotlessly clean and well serviced, always garaged. Then came rural bliss.

The road up to our Shangri-la is paved, steep, and cambered at angles that today would be illegal. My little car, aged beauty that she was, did not find the ascent easy. Once on our short private road, the pavement ended and dust-spewing river rock and dirt were the new challenge. Furthermore, what with hauling animals and plants, the little dowager was losing her luster. It was time for a change, and I decided to sell my little beauty and buy a new, sturdy four-door sedan that I could drive without fear of dents or dirt. My Toyota was and is exactly what I needed; the only dents are those acquired in the Willits Post Office parking lot, which is infamous for careless drivers backing up. The cage would fit.

Once inside, the birds looked at me for some explanation as to what might be their next destination. I assured them that they would love their new home and began saying the names of their new roomies. They, too, would need names. No Big Bird or Ernie, thank you very much. I decided to use the names I would have chosen if I had been able to have children: Zach and Zoe. "Okay, Zach and Zoe, we're going home."

My arrival was marked by the sounds of Blanco barking, Ben following up with his signature woof, and Sarah doing a medley of barking parrot and screaming macaw. The little birds looked up at me, not in fear but in amazement. Another bird? A jungle bird?

I left them briefly in the car while I went inside to figure out where to put them. Perfect. The cage would fit on top of the tabaret, another step down in its noble history—a cage stand. I opened the sliding glass door, and the dogs rushed out to see what was in the car. Sarah stayed on her perch; she must have known that something new was coming into her space. Fortunately, the cage was not heavy, just awkward, and I managed to get it up the stairs and into the house, where it fit nicely on its new stand. The little birds were now officially in shock. Dogs they were used to. A macaw they had not seen since their days in the jungle. Where could they be?

Across the room Sarah's eyes narrowed to pinpoints, then widened to take in the full image of what was sitting in her space. I, as negotiating mother, started explaining to Sarah how much I loved her and what good little birds these were and what fun they could all have together, and on and on. What I didn't tell her, although I'm sure she knew instantly, was that my intention was to let them out of their cage. Not today, not for a couple of weeks until they settled into their new home. But Sarah knew, and I think she would have said "Good work, Nan, good work."

CHAPTER 28

THE "TWINS," as I had affectionately begun to refer to them, were settling in. For the first couple of days, Sarah literally ignored them, much to my surprise. My biggest concern was that the cage was not especially heavy, and I had my concerns that Sarah might be able to move it in some way. True, she could not climb the tabaret, but there was nothing to prevent her from flying onto the cage and potentially knocking it off the stand.

On day three, down she came from her perch, her gaze fixed on the two birds. In the wild, they are not enemies and don't compete for the same food, so I didn't think there was any kind of archetypal enmity between them. But all birds are territorial, and this was Sarah's nest of sorts. When she reached the base of the table, it was clear to her that climbing up was not an option.

What to do? First she pulled at the fabric, hoping, I presume, that she could dislodge the cage from its perch. The little birds looked at me for reassurance.

"It's okay, little guys; it's okay. You're safe; she can't knock you over." My words meant nothing, of course, but my tone must have helped. Sarah gave up on tugging at the fabric and returned to her cage perch. Uh-oh. Was flight imminent?

The little birds must have wondered as well; they huddled closer together and waited for something to happen. Her launch was swift and accurate. With nary a bump she landed right on top of the cage, inches from the birds' heads. One good thing about cages—the bird inside believes it is safe, and so Zach and Zoe didn't look panicked at the leviathan on top of them. Concerned, yes.

"Good bird, Sarah, good bird. Zach and Zoe are good birds, too. We're all going to live together and be very happy. Okay?" For a woman with a strong vocabulary, my animal-speak was smaller than the Dolch list. Still, it's all in the tone, and for that I get high marks. On one occasion, a previous neighbor's pit bull had escaped and found his way into my garden. He wasn't there for the flowers, and I was alone and unarmed. "Unarmed" is a joke; the claw really isn't a weapon. Ben and Blanco were inside, and the door was closed. In the distance I heard the neighbor calling for his dog: "Savage, here, boy." Yes, they had named him Savage; I hoped it wasn't really a character trait. If a person has never been up close and personal with a pit bull, there are two things to be aware of. They're big and they're strong. Their infamous attack reputation depends largely on who owns and trains them. I wasn't feeling especially good about this one's owner.

"Good boy, good boy. What a beauty boy you are. Good dog." I kept up this mantra, and he began to approach. There is something about the term "beauty boy" or "beauty girl" that has some magical, linguistic universality. When I first met Sarah, I called her a "beauty girl"; those two words had a profound effect. If it worked with a vicious macaw, maybe it would work with a potentially vicious dog. He moved closer, and then he pushed his head against my leg. No gobbet of flesh disappeared, so I was feeling better. More "beauty boy," and I found myself petting his head. The look in his eyes told me that he was not vicious, just vanquished. Then the owner showed up and stopped in his tracks when he saw me petting his prime guard dog.

"I don't believe it; no one can touch him, just me." His words made me wonder how he defined the word "touch."

"He's fine." I said, not taking my eyes off the dog's face as his owner came closer. The lead snapped onto his choke collar, and the dog turned away to return to his "home." For weeks afterward, he would escape and hang out in the garden with me.

"No, Nancy." I said to myself. "No more dogs."

Having calmed Savage, I thought I stood a pretty good chance against three birds. Sarah covered every inch of the cage top with her tongue and beak, possibly looking for a way in. Every once in a while Zach would jump up at Sarah's feet, just to show he wasn't afraid. She would hop away from his beak and move to another place on the cage. This went on for at least twenty minutes; finally, Sarah decided that the great outdoors was far more enticing, and she flew to the deck, where she began her journey to the top of the world—the roof.

Alone with my two little friends, I decided to offer them

something to eat beyond their mundane seeds. A couple of almonds, two peanuts, and two shelled walnuts plopped into their dish. Surprised by my gesture, Zach was the first to check out the goods. The peanut went first, then an almond. By now Zoe had come over to the dish, but Zach dispatched her to their perch while he finished the nuts. Eventually, she did get the nuts. It was my first experience with regurgitation. First Zach began to do a little Watusi dance as he resurrected the recent meal. Then he grabbed Zoe's beak sideways, her head below his, and started to deposit his little treat. When it was delivered, he looked pleased with himself and I think also with me. I was grateful not to be on the receiving end.

The next two weeks saw Zach and Zoe become more comfortable with all of the comings and goings of our little kingdom. Neither one tried to bite me through the cage when I fed them, and the look in their eyes now showed light. Kerry was due home the next day, and I had a big decision to make. Should I free them now or wait until he met them? What if he really was upset and I had to find them another home? Once out of the cage, they would probably never go back in. That is a conscious choice for a wild-caught bird owner, and there is no turning back. The newly empty cage becomes an open-door condominium; the key is forever discarded. I wasn't concerned about Sarah. She frequently flew on top of their cage, and it seemed that all three had come to some kind of arrangement. The real issue was Kerry. I decided to wait.

"Hi, honey, I'm home."

It sounded to me like a scene straight out of Desi and Lucy. Red hair aside, she and I have a lot in common.

"Hi, sweetie." I met him out on the driveway so as to introduce him to our newest friends. "I have a little surprise for you, and I'm sure you'll understand." Yes, I could definitely see Lucy's face scrunched in a sideways smile just before she told Desi about the new designer dress. With me it was never clothes. Kerry knew what that funny little face meant.

"What kind of animal did you bring home?" He wasn't upset; motorcycle glow is a very good thing. It's why I encourage him to go off by himself once a year in search of open-road adventures while I adventure around the property. Sometimes it's an animal; other times, it's something in the garden or in the house. It's amazing what a motivated woman can accomplish in two weeks. Lucy would be proud.

"Do you know what a conure is?"

"A little parrot, right? I think Samantha had a pair of them."

"Right. Well, the pet store had these two cherry-headed conures, wild-caught, and I just couldn't bear to think of them living out their lives in that small cage." I knew he would understand. Kerry has the biggest heart of anyone I know, and he had come to deeply appreciate the plight of caged birds, especially wild-caught ones.

"Sure. Not a problem. Where are they?"

"Come on. I'll show you."

It was love at first sight for him, too. He also agreed that we should uncage them, and he did very much appreciate that I had waited for him. Once he settled back in, and with the dogs outside and Sarah up on her cage perch, I went over to their cage.

Reminiscent of the unlocking ritual with Sarah, I opened the cage door and pulled it back against the side of the cage, securing it with a twist tie. Like Sarah, the twins did not move from their perch as I did so. Sarah remembered. She watched every move from her perch. Free to the world, Zach was the first to climb out and up to the top of his cage. Zoe refused to leave, and after a few moments, Zach climbed back inside in an attempt to coax her out. Sarah still had not moved. The next few hours played out much like the first few minutes: Zach out, Zach in; Zoe in, Zoe in. Finally, she braved her way up to the top of the cage with him. Neither had clipped wings, so I wondered if they would fly. The front door was closed. If they did decide to fly, where would they go?

CHAPTER 29

THE WARM, LAZY fall soon gave way to the snows of winter and the seemingly endless rains of spring. The front door stayed closed, and the beautiful light of autumn was replaced by a dark and dreary gray. We were all suffering from cabin fever. I had now lived in this tiny place for ten years, Kerry for seven years before that. Four of those years had been shared with two dogs, two cats, and three birds. I really don't understand what the caged bird has to sing about; I was ready to shriek. Oddly enough, Kerry didn't seem to mind our cramped, often crappy conditions. A country boy of sorts, he's more like a Grizzly Adams or Jeremiah Johnson type who could live contentedly in a one-room cabin out in the wilderness. This was as close as I wanted to get to that scene.

House aside, the property had changed substantially since I had first arrived. The garden had been expanded to include three small ponds, a six-sided fire circle with seating for twenty, a large rose garden with thirty-six different specimens, a southwestern corner with cacti and succulents, many of which bloomed in the spring, and a Victorian gazing garden complete with angel sculptures. There was also the "rust corner" with its assortment of wagon wheel rims, old machine parts, and rusted bric-a-brac—all complemented by orange and red flowers. The Japanese garden was my favorite and surrounded the first pond. Maple cultivars in red and bright green, along with various bonsai conifers, were set off by distinctive boulders and a five-foot statue of Kwan Yin. It was the perfect place to "garden meditate."

The most significant improvement to our place was my office cottage, nearly nine hundred square feet and with its own deck that looks out to one of the oldest and largest madrones in the area. Easily a hundred feet tall, the tree has five main trunks that twist their way to the sky, its crimson and chartreuse bark peeling in the early fall. Inside the office were not only my desk and business paraphernalia but also sofa seating for ten, a Victorian armchair, a small oriental dining table between the sofas, oriental cabinets in teak and bamboo, and a bed for sleepovers. Art that I have collected since my twenties hangs on every wall or is housed in open cabinets. The floor is alive with an assortment of oriental carpets, in anticipation of the day when my husband lays the bamboo floor I bought at the same time I paid him to build the cottage. Like every contractor's wife I know, a wife's building needs are last on his list, because "if he's building something for me, he's not making money." God bless a big commission check that I used to hire him to build my office. Two thousand and two was my move-in date, and move in I did—still lacking the bathroom, the bamboo floor, outside gutters, and finished window trim. Someday, maybe. For now, when the little house became too much to bear, I opted for my cottage, into which no animals were allowed. Even Kerry could enter only with permission. It was my sanctuary.

Winters, however, posed a big logistical problem—bathroom access—so I spent most of my time in the trailer, where tensions always rose as winter wore on. Sarah was no exception. Denied access to her outdoor world, she became peevish and more destructive. Having tasted enough of our furniture, she began to chew on the walls, stripping off large chunks of faux wood paneling and creating slivers that then stuck in the carpet. Kerry and I were constantly on paw patrol to ensure that a fragment of wood hadn't worked its way into the dogs' pads. She also screamed more frequently, including at the television, which we had now begun to monitor. Neither Kerry nor I enjoyed violent shows overall, but we did both like *Law & Order,* along with *CSI.* Sarah would watch along with us, the twins also, and they did respond to raised voices and visual assaults. If the characters registered strong emotions, either crying or yelling, Sarah in particular would respond with her "complaining" squawk, causing the twins to chime in. Physical violence made her sway anxiously on her perch, almost as if the celluloid perpetrator might leap out of the box and attack her. Our typical evening now included censoring our choices based upon bird reactions.

Music was another issue. Kerry's taste is 1960s retro and sailing songs. On occasion, he would play his favorite songs loudly; I would flee to my office until I heard the predictable screams.

"What are you listening to?" I wasn't pleased to have braved the cold rain to return inside.

"Sailing songs; sorry, are they too loud?"

I hate sailing songs, especially when they're played loud, and so did Sarah. Maybe it was that earlier "Peg Leg" epithet, but when the volume went up, so did hers.

"Sarah hates those songs. Can't you listen to those down in your shop?" His shop was at the bottom of our property and only a two-minute walk.

"But I like being in here."

He turned down the volume, though, and once again I trudged back out into the rain. Not for long. Sarah began to scream again, this time because I was leaving her behind in the tiny house with the big sound. She had no way of knowing if he would pump up the volume as soon as I left, so she was screaming for my return to protect her. Back in I went and settled on the sofa, where from all around the walls were closing in.

They were closing in on Sarah as well. The twins didn't seem to mind.

They had never wanted to go outside, so their world was right here, rain or shine. The dogs hated going outside in the rain to pee or poop, but they did it anyway, often opting for the covered deck, which was ever so much closer. Rain or snow, the cats went outside without a complaint. Cabin fever was the hardest on me—and Sarah.

It was mid-March with all of its portents, and the Ides was at hand. We had been enjoying a brief respite from the rain and cold, with temperatures in the balmy sixties. Into the garden I went, bulbs in hand, to dig my way toward spring. I couldn't let Sarah join me because March winds are especially gusty and winds are dangerous for birds. Even the wild birds, ravens and all, stay hunkered down during periods of strong winds. Updrafts can take a bird up too high or too far from its known territory. With Sarah, that could mean the canyon beyond our property or the very tall trees that were everywhere. She had never flown or climbed any higher than about twenty feet. From that height, she could easily climb down, fly down, or fly to another tree, but always at the twenty-foot level. March winds could take her far from her comfort zone and out of my life forever.

That is what had happened to Samantha's beloved cockatoo, Jasmine. For years Samantha would go outside with her little girl, who would perch on her shoulder, then fly about, return to her shoulder, and enjoy her outside paradise. Samantha never took her out when the wind was strong; that last day they went out together, there were no discernible winds. The two of them were on a mesa that reaches out to a deep gorge, with steep granite walls. It is one of the most breathtaking places I have ever seen. At the base of the chasm is a stream that tumbles over travertine rocks and boulders. Flowering vines with tiny red flowers trail up the walls, leading one to believe that this is paradise.

Samantha had begun walking with Jasmine squarely on her shoulder, when suddenly she flew off and up and out—out over the chasm. Samantha ran after her, calling for the bird to return. At the edge of the chasm, she looked for any sign of white wings, but there was none. Jasmine never returned.

That wasn't going to happen to me. Screams I could tolerate;

the alternative was too terrible. So here in March, I listened to Sarah scream while I worked in the garden. The screams became worse, more constant. The dogs were neurotic enough without the added noise level; they hid out in the bedroom most of the time, and Blanco had bitten Kerry. The cats, despite the cold weather, were hanging out in the woodshed, which was protected from the weather. Zach and Zoe reactively screamed in response to Sarah. Our neighbor, Jack, complained. I had become short-tempered, not at all my nature. And the screams continued to get worse. She was wearing me down. What was I supposed to do?

CHAPTER 30

Mood changes as a result of our music and movie tastes continued to bring about more unexpected problems. Another upheaval in our lives was imminent, especially mine.

In terms of location, the television was in one corner of the living room on the lower shelf of Kerry's bookcase. To its right, one shelf up, was my stereo. Kerry's stereo was in the corner of his office and boasted two very powerful Bose speakers that could have sent tunes to Tibet. Because of his schedule, music issues from his corner of our little world were only occasionally a problem. The big problem had become my stereo, whose speakers were much less powerful but were certainly infused with enough bass to thump the chest of any bird.

It was a Saturday, Kerry was at work, all of my work was caught up, and I was in the mood to memory-walk through the last thirty or so years of my life, with music as the stimulus. For the most part, I listen to my favorites at a reasonable sound level. Still, there are certain songs or runs that demand volume to maximize the effect. Today, I laid out my favorite CDs in careful listening order and started my personal hit parade.

First, was Genesis, a concert CD from the early 1980s that kicked off with their megahit "Turn It On." I did, reveling in the memories of where I had been in 1982, who I had been dating, what big successes I had enjoyed, along with the big sadnesses. In order to feed the feeling, I pushed the volume to the point where it cracked the insulation of "Photogenic Memory," another Phil Collins song. Sarah was the first to object.

"Aaacck, aaacck!" Her protests were prolonged and strident.

"It's okay, Sarah, it's okay. Mommy's just rocking out." Those were my words to assure her and the twins that loud music didn't mean there was danger or that I was upset. If my avian trio thought I was upset, it made them very nervous, so I was careful to announce my feelings in such a way that they wouldn't think they had done something wrong or that I was upset with them.

"It's okay, Zachy; it's okay, Zoe. Mommy's having fun." And I was. It was a day to release the stresses of a demanding business conducted in a tiny space with seven little bodies competing for my attention; not including, of course, my own dear husband, whose promises of a house "someday" gave him permission to ignore the one we lived in. Today was just about me doing exactly what I wanted to do. Aaah!

"Aaacck, aacck, aaack!" Phil was losing to the parrot, and stress was working its way back in. I turned down the volume, losing with it the vital pulse of the song. Maybe I should try Dan Fogelberg.

His "Netherlands" recording is one of those that I would take to a desert island if I could have only a handful of favorites. Nineteen seventy-eight was the year of my father's death and that of the only child I was ever able to conceive, the year I began to rethink my life as a fatherless, childless woman. At once uplifting and sad, Fogelberg's songs replay chords long since forgotten. While I don't play him as loudly as Phil Collins, the impact of the emotions is much stronger: "the vision became my release."

What I heard in the parrots' voices was "Why is she so sad? What have we done? What can we do?"

"It's okay, guys; it's okay." But by now my words soothed neither them nor me. The music to afford me release was now frozen in some other time. Maybe it would be best if I found a good movie to watch.

As with my musical favorites, there are movies I watch over and over again. Depending on my mood and where I want the movie to take me, it might be *City Slickers, Saturday Night Fever, Dogma, Michael,* or *Thelma & Louise.* I was in the mood for *Thelma & Louise,* but the last time I had watched that one the birds, especially Sarah, had been mightily bothered by the violence. Given their reaction to my musical choices, I thought I should probably choose a comedy. Perfect. Right there next to *City Slickers* was a video of *I Love Lucy* episodes. Time to go back to the fifties.

Sarah in particular loved these shows. She would dip her head from side to side, looking a little like Ricky trying to figure out what Lucy was up to. Then she would laugh, over and over again. This episode was the one where Cornell Wilde is hiding out in a

Los Angeles hotel penthouse with Lucy's room right below and Lucy is desperate for her hundredth Hollywood star autograph. Determined to get into his suite, she pretends to be a bellboy to gain access to her final celebrity conquest, hides on his deck, gets locked out, and tries to lower herself to the balcony below, only to fall to the ground. She returns to her hotel room, palm fronds woven into her clothes and hair. The episode offers one laugh after the other, and Sarah was laughing so much that it caused me to laugh even harder. Other episodes followed, each one entertaining the birds and making me smile.

Sweet melancholy may have been my original mood of choice, but it was laughter that won the day. I thought that perhaps Sarah didn't want me to feel sad, even if it was nostalgic sadness, so she helped me choose something light.

She was right.

CHAPTER 31

MUSIC AND MOVIES aside, our menagerie was imploding with emotions. We had reached critical mass. Kerry and I looked at each other in desperation. Our best intentions were bringing about an animal Armageddon.

"Hon, I'm really getting worried about Ben. It seems that every time I look, he's licking his paws and acting depressed. He's not the happy Ben dog anymore." I had been the one to carve out our Sunday-morning coffee time, a chance to catch up on the week before the new one started. Much as I liked to keep our conversations light and positive, I couldn't ignore the issue of Ben's "depression."

"I've noticed that, too. He does seem really sad. It also looks like he's putting on weight. What do you think's the matter?"

I guessed he was hoping my answer would hold a solution. Ben was our first baby, and Kerry loved him as much as I did. Instead, I added to the litany of problems.

"Blanco's getting worse with his behavior, too. A spider farts, and he's off on a tirade. He's seeing things that aren't there; I know, because I go outside to check. He's even air biting, especially toward the birds."

"What do you mean, 'air biting'?"

"He menaces the twins and even Ben. So far, not Sarah; but I'm afraid that if he does, her reaction will be to attack him. He's not really trying to bite; it's just his way of saying 'Enough!,' like he did when we first adopted him."

"I think maybe we're in over our heads. Animals are your area of expertise; you have to handle this."

Perfect. He headed off to his shop, leaving me to ponder a solution. Mistoff climbed up on the daybed; Sarah was outside on the deck post surveying the center garden, giving him space to get close to me. That didn't happen very often; and when it did, it wasn't unusual for him to nip at me. This time he was all about purring, and for the time, life was pre-Sarah and calm. Tiger was nowhere in sight. He rarely came indoors anymore, relying as much on wild bird kills as he did on our cat food offerings. The outdoor cats were no less of a loss. All my sweet babies curled up inside various baskets or lounging in the garden beds had become ghosts. It was making me feel as though I wasn't a very good mother and that maybe if I had been able to have children, I might have unwittingly created dissonance among them.

Even Rachel and her brood had gradually begun to disappear from their nightly feedings. We knew that the raccoons had made their nests under the house, up inside the old insulation. Their number had reached twelve before Sarah arrived; recently, I had been lucky to see Rachel with one or two others. She had looked at me with sad eyes, much like Ben's. Somehow I had betrayed her. After only a few months of Sarah's freedom, she left. My calls to her in the evening went unanswered. For a few months more, stragglers would come up on the deck looking for food, but Rachel wasn't among them.

I remembered, wistfully, the first time I had encountered her. She appeared to be wounded, limping on three legs. On a closer look, I could see that her right paw was withered and twisted. A trap, I presumed, from which she had escaped at no small cost to her foot. From the first time I left food outside for her to those moments when she would accept a raw egg from my hand, our relationship had become one of wildness moving to trust. The appearance of her first litter of pups was a miracle to me, and many broods followed. I looked forward to generations of lovable raccoons. Sarah had ended all that.

Sarah was still on her post, beautiful in the sunlight and so happy with her new life. I walked down the stairs to say hello, looking for reassurance that my decisions about her had been good ones, that I wasn't a bad mother. More than ever, I wanted to be able to touch her, to have her rub her head against my arm, to let me pick her up and stroke her feathers. None of that was possible, even though I believed she would have loved me to do so. Her old wounds were too deep, and my new ones were growing.

The only bright spot in all this disintegration was Zachy. While Zoe remained distant, he had become more affectionate and accessible. Just yesterday, I had been adding nuts to his dish, when he brushed his head against my hand. I had frozen, afraid that the tiniest of movements would stop his nuzzling. A few little rubs and he retrieved his almond, held aloft in his claw like a salute. He also "talked" to me, quiet murmurings while he looked straight into my eyes. Then, early this morning while I had been cleaning furniture tops, he had flown at me and landed on my shoulder. Again I had frozen—not only out of surprise but out of fear. My neck offered a rich blood supply, and my ears didn't need further piercing. He just sat there, preening, and for a precious few moments, I experienced the joy of our childhood parakeet, "Happy." From that proximity I could really see his eyes, little golden stars against a dark background. Soulful and just a little sad. What had he left behind in the jungle?

Sarah had been on top of her cage when he landed on me. She rose up to her full two-foot height, pupils pinpoints; she was not happy. Her mate was entertaining another bird. After he flew off and rejoined his bird mate, Sarah climbed down and went outside. Apparently I had produced another splinter in our family timbers.

Kerry was perhaps the biggest casualty of my good intentions and motherly love. He was spending more of his spare time down in his shop, leaving me to manage the children. I was all about placating and very little about peace. The cage was closing in.

CHAPTER 32

As the weeks went by, Kerry began saying "Isn't that cute?" with frustration edged with anger. "What's next?" became more of a challenge to me for a return to gentler times. I couldn't blame him. I was caught in the same vortex of feelings. Despite our basic routines with the animals, each day offered multiple opportunities for disaster—from the crack of dawn, which arrived just before 5:00 A.M., to bedtime, which never came soon enough. Dawn's first light brought with it screeches from Zach and Zoe, who would startle us both out of a sound sleep (although Kerry was sometimes up as early as four o'clock). Not to be outdone, Sarah would add a few screams of her own, and any hope of turning over for a few more winks was definitely dashed. Dressing quickly, I would be the one to let the dogs out for their morning constitutional; then the cats; then Sarah. With the bird on the loose, the outdoor cats scattered like pool balls looking for a safe pocket.

Having the animals temporarily out of the way, I became chef to the critters, and Kerry would lovingly hand me a cup of coffee. I'd try to turn on the *Today* show, forgetting for the moment that it was only five o'clock, two hours before I could attach myself to the New York media lifeline. Out came the ingredients for the bird buffet: kibble, seeds, nuts (three varieties depending on season and price—today, it was almonds, walnuts, and cashews), apples, oranges, bananas, and a tiny clump of granola. Next came cat and dog breakfasts: kibble and a smidgeon of leftovers. Then it was time to wash the water dishes and refill them. Finally, I removed any food left on the bottom of cages or the floor.

Meanwhile, Kerry was busy making his lunch, which ultimately filled a small picnic cooler: two sandwiches, meat of the day; an apple; a banana; two or three ribs of celery; a large chocolate bar; two or three "power bars"; and a thermos of coffee.

"Honey, I really think you drink too much coffee."

"I don't think so; I only drink eight or ten cups a day. That's not so much; and I drink almost a gallon of water."

He doesn't need a truck to get to work; he could get there on his own fuel supply.

By now it was nearly seven o'clock, and Kerry was out the door. The animals were busy playing with the last of their food, and finally I could sit down and watch the *Today* show. The volume was so low that Kerry often wondered if I was indeed human; but that way, I could hear both the program and the clients or editors with whom I was speaking. The birds were quietly preening, the dogs in nap mode. Peace, quiet, order . . .

"No, Sarah, no!" She'd kidnapped Zachy's favorite toy mouse, which he would shake like a predator with its fresh kill. Sarah had predator toys of her own; she also treated them like captured prey. Both Zach and Zoe were now screaming in protest; and of course at that precise moment the phone rang.

"Hello, sorry, who? I couldn't hear you over the birds." My regular editors knew all about the birds by now; they laughed and then repeated themselves. Newer editors needed to learn the drill.

I retrieved the little mouse, and for a few moments everything settled back down.

"Arrf, arrf, arrf!" Blanco must have been barking at a spider because there was nothing and no one in sight.

"Blanco, Blanco, quiet! It's all right; there's nothing there!"

"Aaack, aaack, aaack!" Either Sarah disagreed with me or she was scolding him.

And so it went for the rest of the day. "Hello, hello?" "Aaack, aaack, aaack!" "Arrf, arrf, arrf!" "No, Sarah, no!" "No, Zachy, no!" "Zoe, ouch, ouch!"

It was a miracle I could sell books at all. By four o'clock my stress level was off the charts, and even the tiniest unexpected sound made my heart feel as if it were going to jump out of my chest. I declared my day over and headed for an animal-free zone.

Outside by the pond, I watched the gentle fish swimming without care in their watery world. When I put my hand in the water to feed them, they sucked and nibbled my fingers, even allowing me to pet their backs while they ate. I started to calm down. I started to appreciate how lucky I was to be able to live where I did and to pursue the life that I had here in the beauty of nature.

"Aaaack, aaaack, aaaack!!"

The shrill cry told me that my reverie was over, and I rushed back into the house to see what death or destruction my children might have wrought.

It could have been worse. Sarah was going beak to beak with Zach over God only knows what. Eventually Sarah backed off. Not a surprise; while her big beak is imposing and capable of large bites, his little beak is capable of small, quick bites, and the macaw knew when to withdraw. My intervention was superfluous; I looked at them both and wondered if children would be easier. Probably not, just less poop.

I plopped onto the daybed, gin and tonic in hand. Even when she was on the daybed with me, Sarah had never approached my drink. I did keep a full water glass on the window ledge to "share" with her. This time, she was having no part of water.

"No, Sarah, no. It's not good for you!" A lame statement. I fed her what we ate; why shouldn't she expect to drink what I drank? I'd heard that Winston Churchill's blue-and-gold macaw shared his gin and tonics; and even the Food Network's Paula Deen enjoys "cocktail hour" with her macaw. Perhaps it's an avian tradition; it was about to become one of ours.

Sarah wouldn't relent. A quick judgment call on my part. Would a sip or two hurt her? Bird purists would recoil in horror. But they didn't live in this house. I was willing to risk it.

"Okay, Sarah, just a little bit."

She cautiously dipped her beak into the glass, a wide tumbler fashioned out of very thick art glass, and took her first sip.

"Aaarch!" She shook her head and rubbed her beak against the daybed coverlet. Good, she doesn't like it, I thought to myself. I felt vindicated.

"Hmmm, hmmm!" She straightened her head, and her pupils constricted. Uh-oh. Bird lush in the making.

Back she came to the glass for more. Another sip or two, and she threw back her head in obvious delight. This could be problematic.

"That's enough, Sarah; that's enough. It's not good for you." That last statement was holding no sway with her. Vigilantly, I watched as she took one more sip. That seemed to satisfy her, and she returned to the top of her bamboo perch, where she proceeded to groom herself with a certain self-absorbed relish. I continued to relax, enjoying the rest of my drink. For the next couple of hours it was indeed the peaceable kingdom.

Evening saw Kerry's return from the job site, and the usual husband/wife banter ensued.

"How was your day, hon?" Me first.

"Oh, just fine. We had this . . ." The next several sentences described tools and mechanics for which I had no touchstone; but as every good wife knows, it's all about the listening. My description was no less remote for him; and like a good husband, he listened.

"Well, it was a good day; I worked out the contract . . ." At least his eyes were open.

By now it was time to settle into our evening routine, which meant time for me to start fixing multiple dinners while he sat at his desk and perused the day's mail. For Kerry's dinner, it would be a pasta or rice dish with a side of meat and vegetables. For me it would be lighter fare; my main meal was at lunchtime. Tonight I was having one of my leftovers from the weekend, when I prepare an assortment of meals that I can eat during the week. This one, mok shu, is a delectable mix of grilled red/green/yellow peppers, red onions, black beans, cilantro, and a vinaigrette infused with oregano and garlic. Kerry hated it; too exotic. The birds love it, so each one got a taste from my serving spoon—Sarah first, then Zach, then Zoe. When I got to the pasta for Kerry—tonight, rigatoni with black olives, garlic, Roma tomatoes, and celery—I offered the birds little bites of tomato and celery. The dogs passed; they were waiting for the meat, which I was trimming. The birds joined in, and it was meat trimmings all around. Once the food had been prepared, the animals returned to their own dishes, content.

After dinner, our evening routine was to gather in the living room, Kerry and I on the daybed. There we were, the "animal Waltons," viewing bird-acceptable fare until it was time for bed. When bedtime arrived, it was lights out and good nights to everyone. Back in our bedroom sanctuary, Kerry and I thought about sex ever so briefly. Better not take a chance; mumblings in the "hood." Tomorrow was another day.

CHAPTER 33

ZACH AND ZOE had disappeared. I had been preoccupied with business calls, hours had gone by, and I stopped for a late lunch break. Sarah was on her perch, the dogs were sleeping, and the twins were—where? Probably in their "hood-nest," my euphemism for the bed they had created in the hood of my rarely worn winter coat. Not especially concerned, I decided to make my favorite sandwich: toasted ciabatta with prosciutto, provolone, avocado, and basil mayonnaise. This one I couldn't share with the birds because of the avocado, so I parceled out little veggie bites to include everyone.

"Zachy, Zoe, where are you?" For food they always came flying, Zach to my shoulder and Zoe to the counter's edge. I called again; no response. I covered my sandwich and headed for the bedroom. Could they still be sleeping?

I approached the bedroom slowly, announcing myself as I did so. "Zachy, Zoe, it's me, babies."

Mostly, they didn't attack me, but it was always on a case-by-case basis. No response. I moved closer to the black coat, alert to any movement within the hood. When I saw nothing, I braved a quick touch with my hand, drawing back quickly in case the tiny gargoyles suddenly flew up and out. Still no response. I pushed a little harder, but again nothing. Fearing for my face but determined, I pulled back the edge of the hood and peered into the darkness. They were definitely not in there. As I backed away in bemusement as to where they could have possibly gone, I heard it. A tiny scratching sound, then a muffled mumbling that seemed to be coming from . . . the top drawer?

Impossible! There was no way they could have "done a Sarah" and opened the drawer with their beaks. The scratching sound again, this time with a louder mumbling. I had to look; I had to open the drawer and find out. Before I had the chance, two little feathered bodies appeared from behind the black coat. Quickly scrambling up to the hood, they proceeded to literally yell at me in their best conure screams. What were they? Houdini parrots?

A squawk from Sarah, and they flew back into the living room. I opened the drawer to find shredded papers and handkerchiefs, all that filled the drawer after Kerry had moved some of his clothes into a dresser in his office. Since he gets up very early, he had moved some things out of the bedroom so as not to disturb me when he got up. How had they gotten in there? I pulled back the coat from where it covered most of the dresser top, not knowing what to look for. I found it. There at the back of the dresser surface was a hole the size of a grapefruit, neatly hidden beneath the heavy coat. It must have taken them months to chew that hole into the inch-thick wood; but they had. As quickly as I found their secret, I ran for the living room, the sound of approaching wings overhead.

I continued on into the kitchen, just in case their furious momemtum might not stop in the living room. Sure enough, Zoe was still coming at me; Zach had returned to the perch. Once in the kitchen, the sound of wings over my head stopped as Zoe abandoned her attack. Sarah was watching from the top of her cage with a look that said "Nasty little parrots." On several occasions Sarah had squawked at Zoe when she attacked people, especially me. While they weren't as aggressive with Kerry and me as they were with strangers, those attacks were not predictable. We had become adept at the "six-foot dash" to the bathroom and the "duck and cover" run into the bedroom. Zach and Zoe had never really hurt us, but this new nest changed everything.

What if I hadn't found their secret? Would that have preserved some kind of status quo? Too late for rhetorical questions. This was the new reality.

When Kerry got home that evening, I broke the bad news.

"In the drawer? They chewed through the top and made a nest in the drawer?"

Kerry takes great pride in his furniture workmanship, and up to this point none of his creations had been drastically chewed. This dresser was one of his first pieces; the nest invasion was serious.

"What's next? Every time I turn around it's more mess, more

destruction, more 'We can't do this, we can't do that because of the birds.' I'm sick of it."

He left in a huff to relax in his shop, leaving me to assure all of our animals that everything was all right, that Mommy and Daddy loved them and they hadn't done anything wrong. The wrong-doer was me. As much as Kerry loved and supported my animal passions, I had brought about another tipping point.

I had to find a way to untip.

CHAPTER 34

While I was trying to figure out how to rebalance my life with Kerry, a new twist was about to unfold.

"If I can't touch her, neither can Zach."

At first, I thought it was a strafing attack as I ran from the bedroom toward the safety of the living room or kitchen. The sound of four wings diminished to the sound of only two as I cleared the kitchen entrance. Expecting the sound of those wings to disappear at any second, I was shocked to discover that while the sound of whirring wings had disappeared, the wings themselves had not. The wings were silent, but the feet were talking.

"Zachy, Zachy-man!"

I was shocked. There on my shoulder, looking straight into my eyes, was little Zach. He had landed once before, but immediately flew off. I couldn't move; wouldn't move. If I startled him, would he bite my face; my ear; my neck, with its rich source of veins and arteries? My head was turned only slightly toward this sweet vision of red and green, his eyes so close to mine that I could see the star design of his pupils.

Zoe was still on her perch, Sarah frozen on top of her cage. The little parrot whom no one could touch had chosen to touch me. Why?

I couldn't stand in the kitchen forever, so I decided to move back into the living room, closer to his perch, in case he suddenly experienced flyer's remorse and wanted the safety of Zoe and his perch.

Slowly I turned, step by step, inch by inch . . . an image of The Three Stooges almost brought me to laughter. Not now, don't laugh, don't startle the bird.

As I moved closer to the perch, he changed position and flew. Back to Zoe, back to safety. He had been brave; he had encountered the Goliath. He ruled.

Zoe must have been equally impressed; she began to groom and kiss him like a hero home from the wars. How sweet, how tender, how . . .

"Aaack, aaack, aaack!" Sarah was not pleased. Just because she could not, would not engage me physically, that did not give any other bird the right to invade her "territory."

"It's okay, Sarah; it's okay; he just wanted to say hello. Mommy loves you."

She fluffed her ruffled feathers and looked away from me. There would be a price to pay for infidelity, even if I had not precipitated or encouraged that connection.

Over the next several days, Zach continued to land on my shoulder, which then escalated to his rubbing his beak against my cheek and softly nibbling at my ear. I was euphoric. A wild bird, cruelly captured and confined, had chosen to rise above his captivity and engage me as a trusted being. The euphoria had a growing dark side. Sarah began to lunge at my feet in a mock biting ritual. I no longer felt safe bringing my face close to hers; the eyes said "Beware." Intimacy with the one now threatened intimacy with the other, my chosen significant other.

CHAPTER 35

Kerry and I felt our intimacy eroding, not just sexually but in terms of quality time that didn't include three birds, two dogs, two cats, feral cats, raccoons, and enough poop to fertilize Nebraska. The word "detritus" took on a whole new meaning in our lives; none of our belongings was truly safe, and our self-styled cage rubbed against our backs. A simple kiss from Kerry would bring Zachy flying to my shoulder and Sarah running toward Kerry's feet for a quick bite. We had to get away, even for one night, and remind ourselves that we were human and we were mates.

"Hi, Lori. Listen, Kerry and I have got to get away for an overnight somewhere. If we do that, could you come stay here and watch the animals?" It was a huge request; it meant bringing her four-year-old son and assuming the mantle of "multiple mom." Of course, dear friend that she is, the answer was yes, and Kerry and I happily planned our sybaritic getaway.

CHAPTER 36

KERRY HAD TOLD ME to choose the place, not "fancy" and not too far away, so that we could maximize time in the room. Translation: sex without animals present. My personal preference would have been an ocean view, a room with soft earth tones, damask and linen bed furnishings with Egyptian cotton sheets, and a fine restaurant on the premises. His first choice would have been no view, dark earth tones, any bed covering that kept him warm, and a nearby diner. My choice of compromise was a historic inn only forty-five minutes away, whose little town boasted not only three fine restaurants but also a diner and a pub. The rooms were understated Victorian and the one I chose not overtly feminine. The coverlet was neutral, the blanket warm, the view minimal. I had found twenty-four hours of paradise.

Lori arrived to check in before we left. Food portions were already bagged and tagged; instructions were typed up, specific to each animal's needs. The dogs knew Lori well and loved her; no problem with them. The cats: the usual disinterest. The birds really liked Lori, but they also knew that her arrival meant someone was going somewhere.

"Okay, little babies, Mommy and Daddy are going on a *little* trip; just a *little* trip. We'll be back very soon. We love you."

Postures changed. Heads looked down.

"Bye-bye; bye-bye." Sarah looked up and repeated what she had just said. "Bye-bye; bye-bye."

Kerry and I looked at each other in surprise and with a little bit of sadness. These were new words, precipitated by our leaving.

"Bye-bye, Sarah, bye-bye. Thank you, Sarah." She knew what I meant, and she was content.

CHAPTER 37

Renewed by our little retreat and reassured by the birds' acceptance of our getaway, we decided to throw a party and introduce everyone to our "overextended" family.

The big party was scheduled for the next day. Planning for this one included a rundown of potential disasters and how to avoid them. Kerry was in charge of the outside preparations, and I was in charge of the house.

"Where exactly does Sarah go when she's out here?"

"Everywhere" was not the answer he had hoped to hear. Sarah climbed shorter trees, the willow bench, occasionally the redwood table, the roof, and of course the deck. The party site was smack in the middle of her territory; there was no other choice because of shade issues.

"So how are you planning to protect the food and everything?" Kerry always thought I had all the answers.

As if I knew.

"Why don't we use your worktable with the metal legs? She can't climb it, and with the top covered I don't think she'll try to land on it." Or so I hoped. Our guests could sit in a variety of places, none of which was bird-climbable.

While Kerry rearranged garden furniture and tables and created seating for the expected thirty guests, I was methodically at work in the house.

AREA 1: *The bathroom.* This was the one room most guests were going to need to visit at least once during the party. The back door was right across from the bathroom door, so I decided to tell people to use only the back door for going into the house. Main issue: the conures. Thus far, Kerry and I had been able to access the bedroom with only intermittent overhead attacks; the few guests we'd had had always been attacked. I decided to put a couple of big, floppy hats on the cabinet to the right of the back door. For the guys, any tree would do. The less fortunate women would have to cover and duck. Minor issue: Sarah. We'd have to warn people to keep the back door closed. If Sarah flew to the north of our house, she would end up with our neighbors and their motley crew of dogs. I was ready for Area 2.

AREA 2: *The living room.* Since there was really only the daybed for sitting, I didn't expect anyone to hang out in there. The twins stayed on their perch most of the time, so they shouldn't be a problem. Okay, ready for the kitchen.

AREA 3: *The kitchen.* There really wasn't any reason for someone to come into the kitchen. All the food, beverages, and ice would be outside, so this shouldn't be an issue either. I was feeling much better.

AREA 4: *The deck.* Technically, this was outside and part of Kerry's domain, but I had agreed to secure our extended living room. My self-assurances about areas 1 to 3 began to fall apart. With the front door open, people were going to use it, thus creating potentially problematic foot traffic, which could very well upset the twins. And what if Sarah felt threatened by so many people in her space and became aggressive? Were macaw bites covered under our homeowner's policy?

"Honey, I think we have a problem."

He looked up from his garden tasks with a look that clearly said "What now?"

"I think we can't let Sarah be outside during the party. She could get underfoot or get nervous and maybe bite somebody, or even get hurt herself." One time I had stepped on her when I didn't see her behind me.

"That sure would be much easier. Then we can let our friends see her without having to deal with her, except for the bathroom."

We agreed. His garden work was now done, and I could move to the world of menu preparation. What to serve? Mango-glazed short ribs, grilled of course. Rosemary potato wedges drizzled in olive oil, grilled of course. My family-famous veggie pasta salad with peppers, tomatoes, celery, bok choy, water chestnuts, green and black olives, and cilantro. Yes. The guests were bringing various finger foods, so my menu should be perfect.

Also perfect for birds. No sooner had I opened the refrigerator than the brood showed up. Sarah took her place on the butcher block, making that unusable for chopping. The twins perched on the edge of the buffet; not a problem for prep. Ben and Blanco sat near my feet, moving with me as I walked. Mistoff and Tiger were up on the refrigerator and only mildly curious. Mango for the meat, a piece of mango for the birds. A few slices off one of the short ribs for everyone's pleasure. None of them cared about potatoes, so it was on to vegetables. Under normal circumstances, although normal had long ceased to be a part of my life, my macaroni takes about an hour to prepare. With continuing bird—and dog—bites for each of the ingredients it doubled the time. With everything ready for the refrigerator, my work was done.

The day of the party was perfect in every way. The weather was a balmy 80 degrees after several days of nearly 100-degree temperatures. The food was ready, the garden was pruned and posh with red, orange, and yellow dahlias, which were outdoing themselves this year. The serving table was decked out in a Hawaiian motif with a lei ring for each of the dishes and a striking bird of paradise as a centerpiece. It was the ideal color match to the brilliantly hued dahlias. Even the animals were serenely quiet. Kerry and I hugged each other. This was going to be a great party.

First to arrive were his brother, Creighton, and Creighton's wife, Simone. They had visited only once since the birds arrived, and it turned out to be a very short visit.

"Where are the birds?" Simone asked. Zach and Zoe had strafed her head on her first and only visit, and she looked grateful to be outside.

"They're all inside, Simone; they'll stay in there during the party."

"Good. I brought my own toilet paper; I'll just use the woods if I have to."

Creighton, on the other hand, couldn't wait to go in and see the kids. He loved birds, but he loved his wife more. He had no fear of them, and little Zach would even land on his shoulder. Simone wasn't impressed.

The other guests began to arrive, and within an hour, there were thirty of us reconnecting and sharing good food in our beautiful, bird-free garden. We had specified "no children" out of concern for them with the birds, and the adults quickly got into the bathroom routine—most opting for the great outdoors, where the wild birds lived high up in the trees and didn't visit with humans. Ah, life is good.

First came the banging on the glass, then the screams. Sarah was being deprived of her great outdoors.

"Boy, she's really pissed!" opined the same neighbor who had admitted to calling the sheriff on that "domestic violence" occasion.

"I know. I feel bad, but I'm concerned about everybody."

Suddenly "everybody" suggested that we let her come outside. What? Were they nuts? Here, Kerry and I had done our best to protect them from the raptor they seemed fearful of, and now they wanted her to come outside. True, everyone had made a pilgrimage up to the deck to view her behind glass. Maybe it was the free-flowing wine, but now everyone agreed we should free Sarah.

"Okay, guys, but please don't try to pet her. She'll bite, and you could leave here with one less finger."

I walked up the stairs and over to the door. Sarah's look said "I won; I always win." And out she came. Her descent down the rail made her look like a sideways skier. Everyone was impressed. Her awkward, one-footed gait over to the redwood table made people sigh with sympathy. Her climb up the redwood table made everyone "ooh" and "aah" again. Then she started.

Those sitting at the table had gotten up to accommodate her ascent. Everyone was smiling. Kerry and I were beaming. "How cute," we both thought.

At first she only began to sample the food on the plates. Then it was Creighton's gin and tonic. Oops! I'd forgotten about that. Then it was the silverware, which she flung off the table. Then the plates flew. She had become a one-bird demolition derby. She loved it. Such power over humans!

Our guests looked at us for what to do next. At me, actually, and I hadn't a clue.

"Come on, Sarah, time to go back inside." She looked at me as if I had to be crazy. Outdoors, with all of these admirers? What could possibly be better back on the inside?

Then she flew up to a twelve-foot madrone from which she now looked down upon those admirers. Bobbing her head up and down, she was triumphant. The guests backed away from the tree, partly to get a better look and partly out of fear of falling objects. As if she knew she was onstage, she spread her wings to their full width and lowered her head in preparation for flight. Now I was scared.

She took off—down, thankfully—to a four-foot shrub near the serving table. Now I had a big decision to make. If I left her out here, there was a good chance she might get spooked and fly off. If I picked her up, something I had never been able to do, I would most certainly get bitten. There was no choice.

"Well, people, I need to get her back inside. Give me space here, because I don't know what she's going to do."

"Come on, Sarah; we have to go back inside." My voice was soothing and calm as I approached her. She wasn't afraid of my approaching her, so she couldn't have expected that I would try to grab her. But I did, firmly around her good leg, balancing her on my arm. Only because she must have been startled by my action, she bit me once before I could get her back in the house. The bite was not as deep as it could have been, there on the top of my wrist. It bled only a little, nothing a Band-Aid couldn't fix, and I was back outside with the party. Our guests were impressed with how I had handled her. Kerry was concerned that I was all right. I was in a minor state of shock. I had been able to pick her up. Could this be the beginning of a more tactile relationship?

The party ended on a glorious note of sharing time with family and friends, and of having really touched the bird I so loved.

CHAPTER 38

THE DAY AFTER the party, we all settled back into our routines.

The dogs enjoyed leftover party food; the twins relaxed now that there were no intruders looking for the bathroom, although two of our guests had braved the harpies and survived. Sarah once again had uninterrupted access to both worlds, and Kerry and I turned our attention to cleanup.

"Great party, hon; it was good to see everybody again. Even the birds behaved—well, maybe not Sarah so much." He was pleased to have renewed one of our favorite activities, giving parties that people talked about for a long time.

"It was great. Now we know we don't have to be such hermits."

There we were, sitting at the redwood table, now cleared of

bird projectiles, enjoying the afterglow of time shared with good friends and family. Suddenly a volley of short, shrill barks made us look toward the house for signs of potential trouble. When Blanco didn't come running out in pursuit of whatever had alarmed him, I ran to check things out.

By the time I walked into the living room, the source of the barking was right there. Blanco and Sarah were barking at each other over a bone on the floor between them. Sarah rarely backed down; if she did, it was because something else had gotten her attention. Blanco was usually the one to give in, backing away slowly while still barking in full voice, so as to at least give the impression of partial victory. This time, no one was backing down. The barking was also agitating the twins, who now began to squawk their alarm call. Enough, already. I thought I knew how to solve this one. I gingerly grabbed the bone and tossed it out into the yard.

Surprisingly, out went Blanco like a flash to retrieve his victory treat. Undaunted by the loss of one prize, Sarah turned her attention to Ben, who was gnawing complacently on a twisted rope pull toy.

Sarah walked over to him and pulled at the end of the rope. Ben wasn't ready to give it up and just lay there with two thirds of the toy securely in his jaws. Sarah pulled harder and harder. Now Ben had only half of the toy in his mouth and needed to take more aggressive action if he wanted to retain title. He stood up, feet planted, ready to tug for control. Sarah planted her foot in response; actually, she planted her whole body in response. What a sight! There was a double-wide black dog going nose to beak with a two-pound parrot.

In true dog style, he simply held on to his 50 percent. Sarah was not content with the status quo and began working her beak up closer to his portion, shaking her head from side to side. I had to remind myself that this was a bird. Victory was swifter than Ben expected. Rope toy in tow, Sarah climbed to the top of her cage, where she spent the next half hour or so gnawing on her hard-won prize. Ben, unfazed by defeat, simply found another toy to chew on.

Eventually, the barking, tugging parrot decided it was time to explore the world up on our roof, and out she went. She made it to the flat roof fast, in sharp contrast to her first laborious ascent. I had often watched her climb up the trellis, which secured jasmine, clematis, and roses. Right now, everything was in bloom in shades of white/cream, purple, and yellow. Those colors, along with the heady perfume of the jasmine, made the wall a sensual joy. At the bottom of the trellis Sarah began her climb. The wooden squares of the trellis were perfect for climbing, and Sarah easily reached the flat roof in less than a minute. This morning she seemed to be enjoying the flowers as she went, taking a nip here and there and then tossing the bloom to the ground.

She didn't eat either the jasmine or the clematis, but she had taken to eating the Banks roses, whose individual blossoms were tidy mouthfuls.

I sat there watching her climb and graze, enjoying the serenity of the moment. She was now next to Kerry's office window—which he had left open! In order to control her ingress and egress, only the front door was made available. She had once checked out his large sliding window, and we had agreed to always leave the screen intact.

"Kerry, when did you take off your screen?"

I didn't have time to show how perturbed I was, because Sarah was already climbing into the window. That meant she was inches from all the papers and files on his desk, which were now a beak away from shredding. Since my office cottage had been built, the corner desk had become his.

"Kerry, where are you?"

He had gone back into the house for a late-morning nap and hadn't heard me. Since he is capable of sleeping through a guided missile attack, I would have to be the one to defend his space.

I made the four steps in two leaps and ran for the kitchen, just in time to see Sarah with the end of a blueprint roll in her mouth. Uh-oh. Those blueprints were for a multimillion-dollar home on which Kerry was a cocontractor.

"Sarah, no!" She looked straight at me, blueprints secure in her beak for the moment. Then Blanco showed up. Sarah being reprimanded was worth a trip back into the house. He began to bark wildly at her, as if to say "Yeah, bad bird, bad bird!" It was too much temptation for the barking parrot. She dropped the blueprints and started barking back. Kerry had still not woken up, and I moved the blueprints to higher ground.

"Go outside, Sarah, go play." She finally stopped barking after a minute or so and decided to resume her climb up to the roof. Out the window she went and back onto the trellis. Just as her foot cleared the top of the trellis on the window side, she flipped upside down and thrust her head back into the window.

"Woof, woof. Heh, heh, heh." The perfect avian canine. If the dogs ever grew wings, I knew I would be in trouble.

CHAPTER 39

SARAH'S WINGS were getting plenty of air play. Her flights stayed mostly within the center garden, with occasional forays out toward the pond, where the trees were spaced further apart and she could get more wing time. She had now been free-flighting for almost four years, a marvel to Samantha and others who were afraid to take the chance with their birds. Each day made me feel more and more secure that we were special, we were safe. Sarah was at last a free bird.

"Aaack, aaack, aaack! Aaack, aaack, aaack!"

I had come back into the house, leaving Sarah outside to play as I frequently did. She had now become comfortable enough with the outdoors that being out there by herself was commonplace. Today was the best fall had to offer in our mountains—

80-degree weather and a profusion of red, orange, and burnished copper foliage. The sight of Sarah's blue-and-gold body against this magnificent backdrop was truly a vision of perfection. There it was again . . .

"Aaack, aaack, aaack! Aaack, aaack, aaack!"

A double scream; that meant "serious," and I ran to see what had happened. She wasn't in the central garden, so I headed for the pond, wondering if she might have somehow fallen in. No, she wasn't in the pond.

"Aaack, aaack, aaack, aaack!"

"Sarah, where are you?"

Blanco had joined me in my search and was barking frantically near a small group of trees down from the pond.

"Blanco, where is she? Where's Sarah?" I would have preferred Lassie, but Blanco would have to do.

There, the cry again. I had scoured the airspace up to around twenty feet, the highest she had ever flown. Nothing. Now I was genuinely afraid to look up, but I did. Up, up, up to around thirty feet. Still nothing. Dear God, please don't let her have flown too high. Please.

"Aaack, aaack, aaack!" My ears followed the sound as she continued to scream, and my eyes followed their lead. There she was, in the uppermost branches of a fir tree that had to be somewhere between forty and fifty feet tall. Oh, my God, what was I going to do?

"Sarah, Sarah, it's okay, girl, I'm here. I'll get you down!" How? How in the hell was I going to get her down? I would; I would.

"Come on, Sarah, you can fly down. Fly down!" I beat my

arms as if they were wings, hunching forward as if preparing to launch. She hunched forward in response, squawking as she did.

"There, Sarah, there, that's it. Fly!"

Whoosh. Down she flew to another tree, this one in the thirty-foot range.

"Good girl, Sarah, good girl!" This would work; I'd coax her down to lower and lower trees until she could either fly to the ground or climb back down.

Back in the house, Zach and Zoe were screeching what I presumed was encouragement. Maybe not; maybe it was really "Hey, Sarah, have a good life out there. We'll miss you."

Blanco had stopped barking, and I focused back on bringing Sarah home. I continued to flap my arms and call out my avian cheers.

"Come on, Sarah, come on!"

Whoosh. Down she flew again, this time up toward the central garden, landing in a tree of about twenty feet. Yes! Now we were safe. From that height, she could easily fly or climb down. No, she didn't want to come down. Instead, she began to preen and tug at her feathers, as if recovering from her adventure. She politely ignored my coaxing to come inside and continued to groom. For nearly two hours she stayed on her perch, making me a little nervous. What if her new flight had changed her perspective on living inside at all? Had I lost my beloved bird to a new jungle?

It was still early afternoon, so dusk was hours away. I stayed in the garden, tending to my flowers, pretending it was fine if she wanted to stay up there. My back was turned to her chosen tree as I deadheaded some dahlias. Best just to ignore her and see if that worked. It did. After a few moments, there she was behind me, looking very smug indeed.

"Sarah, you scared me. Mommy loves you; please don't fly that high again. There are plenty of other trees to play on."

She tipped her head from one side to the other, and I swear she smiled at me.

"Heh, heh, heh. Love you."

I wasn't laughing.

CHAPTER 40

KERRY'S MOTHER was finally coming to visit. A remarkable woman in her eighties, she was the kind of mother anyone would hope for.

Kerry had been sharing parrot stories with her for more than a year before she was finally able to come for a visit. She has a pixie face, smiles all the time, and dispenses love like lollipops. No doubt Kerry's loving nature is a gift from her.

"I'm so glad she's coming!" I always enjoyed our visits to Modesto and poring over family memorabilia. She had been to our place only a couple of times since I had moved there, and this visit would be the most special yet because she would get to meet her "grandchildren." In the past, she had met Ben and the two cats, but not Blanco or the three birds. Kerry had been painstaking in describing what to expect from the birds in particular.

"Now, Mom, you don't have to be afraid of Sarah at all, even though she's big. With Zach and Zoe it's a little more difficult. Zachy might try to land on your shoulder, but he won't bite."

"We hope," I thought.

"The problem is, their nest is in our bedroom. They've moved into the top drawer, and now whenever anyone goes near the bathroom, they attack the person's head."

Most eighty-year-old women would have stopped right there; not Kerry's mom. I inferred her reaction from Kerry's response.

"I knew it wouldn't be a problem for you. Can't wait till you get here. Love you."

With that Kerry and I looked at each other with the same thought: "It won't be a problem, right?"

The minute Kerry and his mother walked through the door, suitcase in hand, the birds were on alert. The last time they had seen a suitcase was just before one of my New York trips. What could it possibly mean when a suitcase came into the house with a stranger?

"Hi, Mombee; we're so glad to have you here." She and I had somehow come up with that name as a cross between "Mom" and Bell, her last name. We both liked the sound of it, so it had stuck.

"Oooh, that blue bird is *big*!"

"It's okay, Mom, she really doesn't interact with anyone but Nancy."

So far.

"Oh, and aren't those little ones cute. Can I pet them?"

"No, Mombee; they're wild-caught, like Sarah, and they'll bite. However, lately Zachy has taken to flying on my shoulder; one time he even landed on Creighton."

"Yeah, my brother didn't mind at all; but when Zoe went for Simone's head, *that* was a problem."

I recalled that Creighton's wife in no way warmed up to birds and had alluded to having had some unpleasant experience when she was a child. I hadn't pushed for details.

"Okay, Mom, do you want to sleep in our bed or on the daybed? Either one is fine with us, but the little guys' nest is in our bedroom, and a stranger in there might spook them."

The daybed immediately won, and we set up her suitcase there on the floor, tucked back as far as possible. It had been a long drive, so of course it was time for her to visit the bathroom. I reminded her that Zoe in particular was prone to head razing and offered her a floppy hat to help protect herself, just in case.

"It's okay, I'll just use my newspaper."

With that, she was off to the bathroom, Zoe immediately upon her.

"Oooh, ouch!" The pain was short-lived as the door closed behind her. Getting out would be no less problematic. Zoe was back on her perch, but not for long. Mombee opened the door just a crack and called out to us in the tiniest voice I've ever heard.

"Is it safe?"

"Sure, Mom, just come out quickly."

I didn't realize a woman in her eighties could sprint, but she did; and Zoe rejoined Zach after only one air pass.

"See, Mombee, it's not so bad."

We spent the rest of the afternoon looking at old family pictures and being regaled with Mombee's peculiar stories. Kerry's family boasts some very interesting characters, from Titus Smith, who was commissioned to design weaponry for George Washington, to the founders of both Mt. Holyoke and Smith colleges. My most illustrious family member was Sheriff Ellis, the first sheriff on the Barbary Coast in San Francisco and by all accounts a forerunner of Rudolph Giuliani's New York style.

Sarah continued to ignore us, content, I suppose, that the suitcase didn't seem to be an omen for my departure. When it was time for bed, we all—humans and animals—retired to our respective sleeping places, and the house was calm.

In the morning, Mombee watched in amusement as we shuffled dogs, birds, and cats in our typical breakfast routine. The rest of the day was much like the first; and by the next morning, before she left, it was as if she were a regular member of the family.

"Mombee, it's been wonderful having you here. And you were such a trooper with the birds; you really are amazing."

"Oh, they're not so bad; and it was worth it to spend time with you two. Just one question, Are you planning to bring the birds when you come to visit?"

"No, Mombee, just us." The image of three birds and two dogs in our little sedan made me laugh out loud. Alfred Hitchcock's *The Birds* also came to mind, and I wondered briefly how those birds had been trained. No matter; I had no intention of looking for an animal talent agent for our flock. This house was their stage and we their appreciative audience.

CHAPTER 41

MOMBEE HAD SURVIVED, and the animals hadn't gone ballistic. Now would come an even bigger test. Three of my nieces were coming up to spend the day, and all three were high energy. Jess and Jen were in their twenties; Meghan was fourteen. While not shrill or strident, their voices had a high enough pitch that the birds might react badly. What to expect? How would the birds react to such human cacophony?

"Jess, Jen, Meg! God, it's been so long! You look great!"

Hugs all around, and we went inside to get out of the cold. They had been to the house before, but not since the birds had arrived.

"Wow, those guys are gorgeous!" Jess was the most avid animal lover of the trio and especially loved Ben.

"Ben dog, Ben dog, you are sooo cute!" Ben loved the attention, and then of course Blanco nosed in for his share.

Jen and Meg got into dog hugging, and then we all settled into the living room, mostly sitting on the floor. Sarah stayed on top of her cage, leaving the daybed to Meg and me. Zach and Zoe stayed on their perch, their only concern any movement toward the bathroom or bedroom.

"Can we pet any of them?" Jess again.

"Sorry, they're all wild-caught and they bite. I can't even touch Sarah, much as she loves me."

"That's so sad." Jen this time. "How can people hurt animals? It just makes me furious."

Meg, always the practical "old soul," asked a different question: "How long do they live? I heard that parrots can live to be a hundred. What happens when you and Kerry die?"

Ah, yes, the long-life question. Kerry and I had discussed that one, since the odds were that all three birds would outlive us. Sarah, in particular, could live into her eighties; conures have an average life span of forty or more years. At our age, we would be leaving behind kids with no way to take care of themselves.

"Well, Sarah could live to be eighty or more; did you know that Winston Churchill's blue-and-gold macaw is still alive at the age of one hundred? And a breeder friend of mine in Texas had a scarlet macaw who was one hundred and ten."

"Holy shit! Nan, all of these guys are going to outlive you." Jess seemed deeply concerned. "Who's going to take care of them?"

"Kerry and I don't know. We would never sell them; besides, no one will want birds that can't be caged. Even if someone managed to get them back into their cages, I'm convinced they would die of double grief—first, losing us and then their freedom."

A small silence and Jess spoke up, quickly followed by Jen, who echoed her offer. "We'll take them. Put it in your will, and we'll make sure that the rest of their lives are happy."

I was shocked and immensely relieved. "Really, are you sure?" I sounded like Thelma and Louise just before they drove over the edge of the Grand Canyon. "I can't thank you enough; I would also leave ample money for their care. You are both extraordinary women."

Women; that's right, they were women. They were no longer the little girls who had nicknamed me "Roo" because I had given each of them a stuffed kangaroo, complete with baby in pouch, when they were seven. To them at that age, and even as they got older, I was always the Roo, a woman who was mostly child and who loved animals more than almost anything else.

"You guys—you, too, Meg—are the best. If I could have had children, I would have wanted you as my daughters."

More hugs, more funny stories, more boyfriend advice, and then it was time for them to go. The birds had been remarkably quiet, almost as if showing respect for these strangers who had offered to look after them. No one had needed to use the bathroom, so there had been no Zoe raids. The day ended on a loving note.

"We love you, Nan. In a way, you are like our mother. Give Kerry a hug for us."

With that they were gone and I returned to my own A. A. Milne story, back to my little Roos.

CHAPTER 42

SUNDAY, MARCH 15, brought 70-degree weather and a day to myself on the property. Kerry was visiting his mother in Modesto, and all of our kids seemed especially calm. All except Sarah. For the past few days, with the weather so clement, the dogs had been going outside, but the front door had remained closed. I was once more in the garden, planting and pruning, with Sarah screaming in the background. "What could be wrong with my human?" she must have been thinking, when she could clearly see that this was outdoor bird weather.

There wasn't any wind that I could detect, just a very occasional light breeze that lasted but a moment and was gone. Perhaps it would be safe to let Sarah come outside after all. I waited until midday, just to reassure myself that no sudden winds would kick up unexpectedly. Calm until noon, so would follow the afternoon. While Sarah was in midscream I opened the door, full and wide like the first time I had let her out. She tilted her head from side to side, seeming to ask if this was a trick or the real thing.

"Come on, Sarah, let's go outside. Good girl."

With that she was out the door, up the post, down the railing like a skier with a gold medal at stake, down the post, and skedaddling over to the trellis. She bested her one-minute average in reaching the roof, with not even a quick glance at the closed window. She was Annapurna-bound.

Up on the roof, she stretched tall and spread her wings. "Ah!" she must have said. "Finally, freedom."

"Okay, Sarah, you enjoy the roof and I'll enjoy my plants." With that, she began to drag her beak across the surface like a little vacuum cleaner, refreshing her memory of the roof's sights and smells. No one else went up there, so it was all about her. I watched her traverse the entire space, making sure, I presume, that no intruder had trespassed upon her domain during her absence.

Now it was quiet. My heart wasn't playing mad racer to every untimely scream. Zach and Zoe were silent, the dogs were napping, and I was in a glorious moment of calm. After planting, I meandered to each of my garden spots in search of surprises. At the first pond it was a tiny green frog balanced perfectly in the middle of a calla lily leaf. At the second pond it was an iridescent blue dragonfly hovering over the water. In the third pond, a gold-and-white butterfly koi must have mistaken the warm weather for spring and had come out of hibernation for just a moment or two before the water temperature told him it was a false call. In the Japanese garden, the maples were budding out while the conifers sprouted little cones. From place to place, I walked without purpose, open to every serendipity.

Up in her aerie, Sarah was her best happy self, looking out over her kingdom. "It's good to be the queen," I could almost hear her thinking. Mel Brooks would have smiled.

The rest of the afternoon went on in the same languorous fashion. No winds had arisen, and I was grateful beyond words to the universe that had given me this beautiful, peaceful day.

"Time to go inside, Sarah. Come on, girl." It was nearly four o'clock, and light was fading among the trees. I walked toward the deck, looking up to see exactly where she was on the sixty-foot roof span.

"Come on, Sarah; come on, girl. Time to go inside."

Surely she was preserving every moment of freedom before she had to return to her interior cage. In a moment or two, there she was, perched on the edge of the roof directly over the deck below. She bent over as far as she could without falling, as if to say "Not yet; I'm not ready yet."

"Come on, Sarah. It's going to get dark soon. You have to come inside."

My tone must have communicated that she really needed to come down, so she hunched her wings for flight. Down she came, toward the center of the garden and then—up. Up across the open space at the front of the property, up into an eighty-foot fir. That line of firs was the last "fence" before the canyon opened up beyond.

"My God!"

I ran to the tree where she had landed, calling for her to come down as I ran. From the base of the tree I could see her looking quite comfortable on a leggy branch that gave her a very different view of her outside world. She was twice as high as she had ever been. I wondered how different things must look from that height. A dahlia would become a forget-me-not. The redwood table a stool. The trailer, her roof, now the size of the center garden.

"Come on, Sarah; come down, girl." While I couldn't see the expression on her face, her posture told me that she was not frightened. She must have been curious, but she certainly wasn't scared. I spent the next twenty or thirty minutes watching her watching everything. By now the sunlight was gone and deeper darkness was only an hour away.

"Come on, Sarah, come on. It's getting dark, baby." If I couldn't coax her down before dark, there was no choice but to let her sleep in the tree. She wouldn't try to fly down at night, and there were no nocturnal predators at that height. We did have owls, but she was too big a prey for an owl. Strangely, I wasn't too scared. Stories abound about birds who have spent a night outside, then come down the next day. Besides, she had been a wild bird. Wild birds fly. Wild birds know how to get down out of trees. In our garden, she had been a prolific climber and flyer. It would be fine. She'd be fine for one night. The weather was warm, no rain in the forecast. Everything was going to be all right. When I spoke to Kerry on the phone, he agreed.

"Don't worry," he said. "She's a bird. Birds fly, up and down. She'll come down tomorrow."

His words reassured me. Yes, she'll come down tomorrow.

CHAPTER 43

DAY 1

Tomorrow came and with it a sense that everything would be all right. The temperature was dropping, and rain was in the forecast; I hoped it would hold off for a while. Branches become slippery when they're wet, and she had only one foot. I thought, what if she fell? No, she's a bird; she'll be fine. That morning, I called our friend Connie, whose conure was always escaping from the house and flying off for a day or two. Each morning, Connie would place food and water in plain sight of the trees around their garden; and sure enough, the bird would manage to fly down, housebound until her next escape. Samantha, while not as confident as Connie, echoed the same thought: Sarah was a wild-caught bird; she'd find a way down.

We heard nothing from Sarah during the night, nor would we

have expected to. Calling out at night in the jungle would have been tantamount to extending a dinner invitation to predators. At first light I was out by the tree, where Sarah was sitting in the same location she had been the day before.

"Come on, Sarah, come on." Over and over again, I kept urging her to fly down. She could do it; I knew she could.

Hours passed, the same words over and over again, and still she sat. The temperature was continuing to drop, and rain was only hours away, at best. A slight wind picked up, and I hoped that might encourage her to loft and fly.

A sudden low hunch and she flew—straight toward the garden and then up across the roof to a hundred-foot fir behind the pond. I watched, convinced she would choose a lower branch from which she could negotiate a flight down to the ground. Instead, she landed maybe eighty feet up, but there were lots of little branches all the way up and down the tree; she could climb down. I had run nearly as fast as she flew and looked up at her from the base of the tree.

"Good girl, Sarah! Good girl!" She would get down; yes.

She looked around at her new perspective on the world. This tree was on the edge of the most extensive and densest forest on the property. Her only clear perspective was back across the roof, to which she had an unobstructed view, and back across to the center garden. After several aborted flight attempts, she tried to climb down. The lower branches were thinner than the ones closer to the top and were spiked with smaller twigs that made climbing down problematic. A couple of launches and she stopped; instead, she climbed up even higher, where the footholds were stronger.

"No, Sarah, no! Climb down, climb down; you can do it!" It was now nearly dusk, and rain droplets had already begun to fall. If she didn't get down today, at least she would have water. The branches, too, were thick; the shelter wouldn't be too thin.

"Okay, Sarah, I have to go inside now. I love you."

Back in the house, Zach and Zoe looked especially concerned. "See," I could hear them thinking, "the world out there is dangerous; we're staying right here, where it's warm and we get all the food we want." The other animals were more concerned with my state of mind—i.e., will this affect our needs? Kerry was working long hours on his new project, and so far it didn't seem that he needed to pitch in. The day ended on a still-hopeful note. Tomorrow would be the day she came home.

DAY 2

It had rained all night, hard at times, and the morning temperature was only 34 degrees, not quite cold enough to snow but cold enough to make the freezing rain bite. Kerry asked if I thought he should try to help, but I was confident that today would be the day.

"It's okay, hon; she's made a lot of attempts to fly, and I think the rain will help to motivate her to get down out of the tree before the weather gets any worse." With that I was out of bed and back to my tree vigil. I looked like a northeastern fisherman out for the morning catch in foul weather. I felt as though I were carrying an extra twenty pounds of clothing, although I'm sure it was more like seven or eight. Regardless, I was out there with my mantra and my faith.

"Hi, Sarah, how are you, girl? You must be so cold and wet. Come on down. Come on, you can do it." She was in roughly the same place as she had been last night. Even from that height she looked bedraggled and wet. She simply must fly down.

More hours passed; the rain was steady, and I had started to take little breaks back into the house. When she still wasn't down by noon, I called my friend Lori.

"Sure, Nance, I'll come over and help."

Sarah liked Lori and allowed her to feed her without trying to bite at her. Not even Kerry could do that. She was there in a few minutes, and I told her my plan.

"I'm going up on the roof. It's the only clear view she has, and it's familiar. Maybe she will fly to me and I can help break her landing."

"You're crazy. First of all, it's raining. Second, the roof is likely to be slippery. And last, remember you're afraid of heights *and* you'll have to climb a ladder! It won't work."

"That's why I called you. If you hold the ladder, I think I'll be okay. Then if I panic when I get up there, at least you can call for help. I have to try, Lori; she's not coming down on her own, no matter how hard I coax her."

Sarah definitely noticed that we were up to something. Ladder in place, up I went, fearful with each step. When I reached the roof, I pulled myself over the top in a sort of roll-and-tumble maneuver that put me facedown on the roof. I stood up and walked to the center of the roof, so as not to see the drop from any of the edges. I walked as far as I could to the edge facing Sarah, probably three feet from that edge. Sarah became visibly excited.

"Aaarck, aaarck, aaarck!!!" Now her head was bobbing up and down and her wings were moving up and down in rhythm with her head.

This was it! This would work!

"Good girl, Sarah. Fly, Sarah, fly!" I flapped my arms, feeling a little like a mother bird trying to convince her fledglings that their wings can carry them out of the nest.

"It's working, Nancy, it's working! She's going to fly down!"

And for the next three hours, it continued to look as if she were going to fly down, me flapping my arms and doing my best impersonation of a desperate mother bird.

By four o'clock I was still on the roof and Sarah was still on her perch. The rain was becoming dangerously heavy, and I needed to go back down. I went to the edge where the ladder was and I backed down each step, too tired to be as fearful as when I climbed up. Lori and I hugged, and home she went. I went over to the tree and said my good nights to Sarah. My hope was draining.

DAY 3

Kerry took the day off after hearing of my roof escapades the day before.

"I know this professional tree climber; he's a tough little Norwegian who used to work ship masts. If anyone can reach Sarah, he can." I agreed enthusiastically. Today would be a good day, despite the continuing rain.

Carsten arrived with full climbing gear, confident that he could retrieve Sarah. He suggested that he carry a small net, which he had brought with him; this wasn't the first bird he had rescued from a tall tree. Kerry and I took him out to where she was, and he looked up, unfazed by her position or height.

"Not a problem; I've climbed taller trees than this one. I'll get her down."

Confidence was restored. Today would be the day. Up he went, spiking his way up to within ten feet of her in mere minutes. He looked back down at us on the ground. "Don't worry, I'll get her."

He moved slowly for the next few feet, presumably not to spook her. When he was within four or five feet, he carefully retrieved the small net from his belt. At the sight of the net, she flew—not to a lower place but back into the dense forest behind her. I gasped. Now what?

Carsten climbed back down, determined to climb whatever tree she had chosen in order to recover her. And so the rest of the day went. In all, Carsten climbed seven trees before he gave up. Now Sarah was not only stranded; she was being hunted. The day ended on a profoundly sad note. What to do next?

DAY 4

Kerry took another day off from work. We had made a decision: If we can't climb, we'll cut. The rain had stopped and wasn't expected to return until late that night, or perhaps the next day. Kerry called two of his friends, and the tree-cutting campaign began.

First I located Sarah in the dense forest; then Kerry and his men assessed the best way to access her tree. In all, over the next nine hours, we cut down at least twenty trees. With each felling, Sarah flew to another tree, out of reach. At the end of the day, we had savaged our forest and failed to bring Sarah home. I told her good night and returned to the house, feeling as broken as those felled trees. Kerry, too, was depressed and suggested that perhaps we should call the California Forestry Department or the local fire department the next day. We had nothing to lose. The rain returned that night, with a vengeance, and we slept little.

DAY 5

By noon on the fifth day, our driveway looked like a government parade: fire trucks, forestry vehicles, a crane, and twenty or more personnel. Once they had assessed our situation, their overall evaluation was that the bird would come down when she was ready. Still, and because Kerry and I have friends in high places, they were willing to give it a shot. That shot lasted almost three hours before the phalanx of trucks returned to their government nests, Sarah still perched in a too-tall tree.

Kerry decided to put in a partial day on the job site, and I was left to talk to Sarah for the rest of the afternoon.

"Come on, Sarah, come down. You can do it!" My tone was more demanding, something along the lines of "Why don't you just fly the hell down here; you're a bird, a wild bird!"

If I was beginning to lose hope, so was she. I could see it in her posture. I needed a break and went back into the house.

Because the rain had let up and the sun had provided some temporary warmth, I had left the front door open so that the dogs could enjoy some freedom. Zach and Zoe stayed on their perch, noticeably upset by the continuing commotion.

"Hi, guys. Momma loves you. You're good babies." They needed to know that I loved them and that they were not in any kind of danger.

I walked toward the kitchen, not really caring about fixing dinner, when *whoosh!* What was that? It was Zoe, timid Zoe, on her way out through the front door and on to Sarah's "first tree" in the center garden.

What?

There she sat, not frightened but free, while I watched in disbelief. Should I close the front door? No, I had to coax her back inside. Zach called to her to return; I had come to know those "words." Zoe called back, but hers was an invitation to join her in the free world. He wanted no part of it. She stayed on that tree for perhaps an hour, then flew off. Zach continued to call for her for hours; she never returned. What I believe is that she wanted to join Sarah, that somehow Sarah's escape was a call to action for her. That night, I went to bed having lost two of my children.

DAY 6

By now everyone in the neighborhood and out into our community knew about our lost birds. Calls came in about sightings of a "brightly colored bird" in various locations throughout Willits and Ukiah. None of them amounted to anything, and I thought of all the parents whose children have gone missing and for whom hopeful calls only deepen the pain.

Zoe had not returned, and I continued my forest forays to locate Sarah's most recent tree and try to talk her down. I was losing all faith. My business had come to a standstill; my eyes were swollen into slits; and the mood around the house was grim at best. I was praying for a miracle.

DAY 7

The next tree was behind our house to the north. Sarah's voice had deepened to a kind of throaty whisper. Her feathers looked sodden and dull from all the rain. My entreaties continued, but it was almost as if both of us knew the odds were against us. By evening she flew one more time to a tree I could not locate. I could neither hear nor see her. It was the darkest night of my soul.

CHAPTER 44

IT WAS NOW the eighth day since Sarah had flown up into the trees; six of those days had been cold and rainy, with nighttime temperatures down into the thirties. Yesterday had been my last sighting of her high up in a fir tree behind our house on the north side, the coldest of all locations. I had been out walking and calling despite the rain, having lost sight of her when she flew from her then current tree into a dense pocket of firs and madrones. I was still amazed that a bright-blue-and-gold creature could so easily disappear into the foliage, but she did.

If it hadn't been for her calls, I might never have seen her at all. My ears had become antennae that could distinguish direction and height. Those who had been helping us look for her were convinced I was morphing into some kind of nonhuman animal.

There she was, probably eighty to ninety feet up, and her flight possibilities from this present tree were primarily to the south, over or around the house. I hoped she would opt for the house route, because she might be able to crash-land on the roof she was so familiar with. I knew it would have to be a crash landing, and with her one foot it could be deadly. Did she know that?

"Come on, Sarah, come on down. You can do it, girl. You can do it."

Every time I said those words, they sliced into my heart. The hopeful tone from days earlier was now steeped in growing despair; I knew she could sense that. I noticed that her posture had changed from the last time I had seen her. She no longer held her head up; the posture of her body was downward. She was giving up, so I couldn't. "Sarah, you can do it! Come on!" She did not respond at all to my words. No more raised wings or bobbing head or preflight hunches. She just sat there.

It was now so dark that I had to use my flashlight to say good night to her. I walked back to the house with a sense of impending doom. The dogs felt it, even the cats. Kerry just gave me space; he knew from my mother's recent death that I prefer to grieve alone, that offering me solace only weakens my resolve to do whatever has to be done. Like cracked glass, I would be too easy to break if anyone held me. Zachy was the most depressed of all the animals. He was hardly eating, and he almost never left his perch. Even his posture was hunched. He was grieving, too.

"Hi, hon. No luck, I presume." His words were gentle but not helpful.

"No, she's just sitting there, waiting for a miracle, I suppose. I don't have one."

"Well, while you were outside, a woman named Charlotte called about a scarlet macaw she needs to find a home for."

"I can't think about another bird right now! How did she get my name?"

"Beryl down at Tropic Tails told her about you; she also told her that your blue-and-gold was missing and that you would be the perfect new mother for her bird. Here's her number."

I looked at the numbers, and they danced around in a blur of tears. How absurd! It felt as if a loved one were on her deathbed in the next room while I romanced a new one in the living room. No, I couldn't do it. Sarah might somehow get back to us.

"Why don't you at least call her? She's desperate because her toddler is now old enough to poke around the cage and it's only a matter of time until he gets bitten. Sounded like she really loves this bird. Go ahead, just call her."

I picked up the phone, ready to dispatch this woman's request with a tear-soaked voice that would surely let her know that I couldn't possibly adopt her bird.

"Hi, Charlotte, this is Nancy calling you back about the bird. Yeah, listen, I'm just in too much pain right now to even consider adopting your bird. I'm sure he's wonderful, but I just can't."

She went on to explain how she had "rescued" him from a pet store because he was miserable in his too-small cage and because she loved his antics, especially the way he would dip his head down from one side to the other, all the while saying, "Hello, Will, hello." His name was Will Scarlet, so named by his first owner, who had given him up after only one year. Charlotte had had him for two years, and they were inseparable. She had bought him the biggest cage available, but she also let him out regularly. He didn't bite, he was affectionate, and he had a sense of humor.

A sense of humor! Her description was beginning to wear me down. I could use a little humor right now; and besides, seeing such a beautiful creature might be a good thing for me to do.

"Okay, you've won me over. How about tomorrow?" With that, I went to bed, my dreams full of Sarah and some unknown red parrot named Will Scarlet.

CHAPTER 45

I ARRIVED AT Charlotte's house around noon. It was a small house—not as small as ours—but it was cozy and furnished with "man furniture": two big recliners, a brown leather sofa, and big clunky end tables with mismatched lamps in the living room; I could only guess at the bedroom. The oldest of her two children was in the master bedroom watching the toddler. She and I were alone in the small, crowded kitchen with its Formica dining set, limited counter space, and a huge cage.

There he was, and he was splendid. He was slightly larger than Sarah; his beak was ivory white, not black; and he was not masked like the blue-and-gold. His coppery eyes were set into a pearl white face without the blue-and-gold's black bars. His feathers were predominantly bright red, offset by a ribbon effect of green, yellow, orange, and turquoise feathers. He was the most beautiful bird I had ever seen! Then yesterday's vision of Sarah in her tree stopped me cold.

"Charlotte, he is amazingly beautiful, but I just don't know. Isn't there anyone else to adopt him?"

"Well, originally, I was asking $1,500 for both him and the cage, but I haven't liked any of the people who came to look. Neither did he. After talking with Beryl, I've decided that if Will likes you, he's yours for free. I really can't 'sell' my child."

Another free bird? Right!

With that she opened the cage, and he stepped up on her arm. He climbed up to her shoulder and rubbed his face against hers. She offered him a pistachio, and he took it without biting. She petted his head and back, and he raised one wing to its full span as if to say, "Thanks, that feels good."

"Here, why don't you hold him?"

Could I, should I? I put out my arm and asked him to step up. He did. His claws needed to be trimmed, and it wasn't all that pleasant, but I was holding him.

"Hi, Will, my name is Nancy, and I love birds. Do you want to come home with me?"

I couldn't believe I was saying these words, but I was absolutely caught in the moment. He inclined his head toward my face. My, that was a large beak, easily 20 percent larger than Sarah's. He extended that beak closer to my face, toward my mouth. Dared I even try this? What if he chose to bite my tongue, instead of kissing me?

I extended my tongue in a gesture of faith and hope. Very gently, he tickled the end of it with his own tongue; then he pulled back, looking satisfied.

"I've never done that with him!" Charlotte was testing me; her own fear of being bitten had kept her from ever trying to kiss him.

I had brought a little bag of chicken wing bones, the kind Sarah loved, and decided to offer one to him. He took it delicately, without biting, and proceeded to bite and lick his way into ecstasy.

"They eat bones?" Charlotte was amazed. She had obviously never explored his raptor side.

"Yes, they love them—and lamb bones and beef ribs. They're definitely little carnivores."

As we watched him chew bone after bone, we discussed his behavior and other relevant details about his history. He had been domestically raised and hand-fed. In that regard, he was nothing like Sarah. In other ways, he was a lot like Sarah—taken from his breeder by a new owner, abandoned, caged, sold to a new owner, and now ready for another new home.

"I think I must be crazy, but I'll talk to my husband and consider taking him. I'll let you know tomorrow."

"Oh, I'm so glad! I really hate to give him up, but I have no choice. I know you'll be the perfect mother for him. Please, I hope you decide to adopt him."

With that I drove home, planning to talk to Kerry that evening. I knew he would say that I should adopt the new bird; it would be more of a courtesy between us. The rain had cleared, the sun was shining, and I was tempted to go out one more time in search of Sarah. I got as far as the big fir tree behind the pond, and I broke down. I didn't know that humans were capable of howling. They are. For what seemed like an hour, I keened until I was nearly hoarse. She was gone. Maybe not dead, maybe to some other wild flock or some new solitary life, but she was gone.

That night, I had my third dream about Sarah since she had flown off. In the first, her feathers had been ratty, but she was drinking water and telling me I shouldn't worry. In the second, she had been leathery and dry, more skin than feathers, and her eyes were empty orbs. This time she was only bones; beautiful, pearly white bones through which shone a warm, yellowish white light. There was a joyful aura around her; then she told me to look "over there": A red bird, a parrot, and I awoke with a start.

I was going to adopt Will Scarlet.

CHAPTER 46

THE NEXT MORNING, I called Charlotte and told her the answer was yes and we would pick him up the following weekend. She thanked me tearfully; we both knew that Will Scarlet would love his new home.

For the next few days I turned my attention to life, not death, and focused only on what had to be done to prepare for Will's arrival. In truth, there were no preparations to be made, but I created scenarios in my mind about what it would be like to live with the new bird. Kerry and I decided to put the cage right in front of the living room window where the daybed had been; a new sofa now faced out from the opposite wall. The bamboo screen was secured at a right angle to the window wall and was still a perfect climbing perch. Of course, this would mean removing Sarah's cage from the house. That would be a very sad occasion, but we would do so at the very last minute before we went to pick up Will. If by some miracle Sarah did return, we would somehow turn our little house upside down to create enough room for three cages.

I started using Will's name with the other animals, in particular Zach. Since Zoe had disappeared he had become severely depressed and had begun to pluck, something male parrots do to attract a mate or if they are upset. His little chest was no longer covered with bright green feathers, only gray and white down. In some places the skin showed through, but there was nothing we could do. Perhaps the new bird would offer him needed companionship. I wanted all of them to recognize the new bird not as a stranger but as a family member.

Thoughts of Will were indeed brightening my spirits. And in some odd way, as long as there was no habeas corpus for Sarah, I could harbor the hope that she might have survived the bad weather and found a way to live free and wild somewhere else.

The day before we were to pick up Will, Kerry was in his shop working on a project and I decided to walk down and take him lunch. More sunny weather, warm, and I was feeling good about this new bird. Like the rest of our property, his shop is surrounded by numerous tall trees, mostly firs. I walked leisurely, feeling lighter than I had in the last two weeks. Something at the base of the fir nearest Kerry's outside storage area caught my eye. Probably a blue jay, poor little guy. I walked closer to see; it wasn't a blue jay. It was Sarah.

I screamed and dropped Kerry's lunch. Kerry came running outside to see what had happened. There I was, kneeling on the ground next to her lifeless body. In a way, she looked as if she were sleeping. There was no blood, no visible sign of anything broken or mangled. She was just lying there, on her side, eyes shut and dead. I had to touch her to be sure. The body had gone past rigor mortis but was not yet into decomposition. She had probably died within the last day or two, but how?

I picked up her body, able to touch her only in death. How soft she was! I had no idea. I could feel her bones through the feathered flesh. Perhaps she had starved to death. Maybe the weather had caused her to die of exposure and then she had fallen to the place where I found her. My thoughts started to blur; the tears frozen by the first sight of her became a torrent.

Kerry just stood there quietly. He didn't try to touch me or offer any consoling words. There weren't any to be offered. All he said was "Let me know if you want me to do anything; I'll be in my shop."

I nodded and stood back up with Sarah in my hands. How strange, there were no bugs or maggots. She almost looked alive, but of course she wasn't. I walked back up to the center garden and placed her on the redwood table. There were no thoughts, no memories in my head. Just blankness, emptiness, a void where she had once been. I chose to bury her out near where the new pond would be someday. I dug the hole with my garden claw, just as I had dug all the holes with her during bulb season. The hole had to be deep, nearly three feet, so that other animals wouldn't dig up her body. When it was deep enough, I placed her in the hole, surrounding her with all of her favorite toys, including a couple of rib bones. I replaced the dirt with my hands until the ground was smooth and flat. On top of her grave I put the onyx sculpture of a macaw that a friend had given me for a birthday gift. I stood up, said good-bye, and walked back to the house.

Zachy looked at me in a way that told me he knew I had found her. I went into the kitchen and fixed a too-early gin and tonic. I went back out into the garden, to the first tree she had ever climbed. I toasted her and wept. Those dreams had been true. Now it was time for the red parrot.

CHAPTER 47

I HAD FOUND Sarah's body only yesterday, and now it was time to pick up Will Scarlet. Charlotte had waited the extra time because she knew I wasn't ready to embrace a new bird so quickly; now time was working against her as her toddler became more fascinated with Will's cage. If I didn't take him, she would have to sell him to somebody else or let our local pet store broker him. I needed to bring him home.

Kerry was both supportive and sympathetic. Since Sarah had never really adopted him, he didn't feel the same pain of loss that I did; but he did empathize with my pain. The day before we went to pick Will up, we moved Sarah's cage outside near the gazebo and future pond site. Inside the cage I put the stuffed macaw that Creighton and Simone had brought back to us from

New Zealand. Ironically, it was a scarlet macaw instead of a blue-and-gold. The cage sat forty or so feet from her actual grave; I wished that I had buried her next to it. Kerry offered to exhume her, but I couldn't bear it. No more tears, no more tears; I had to welcome Scarlet with a smile.

Will knew he was leaving Charlotte and his current home. Kerry and I arrived in his truck so that there would be enough room for me to hold the portable cage on my lap while his large cage was secured in the truck bed, along with his freestanding perch. We knocked, and from outside we could hear Charlotte telling him that it would be all right. I could also hear the tears in her voice, and it helped me to squelch my own. "Hi, Charlotte; this is my husband, Kerry. We're so excited to have Scarlet become part of our family."

Scarlet was out of his cage and perched on the arm of a recliner. He knew.

"Hi, Will, remember me?" I walked over to him and petted his head and back. He bristled slightly, not knowing for sure what would happen next. I offered him a chicken wing bone, just as I had done the first time I met him. Snap, crack, suck the marrow. I gave him another and another while the three of us discussed the logistics of how to get the cage out of the kitchen and into the truck. Then we briefly discussed his health record while I continued to feed him bones. By the time the floor around his perch resembled a prehistoric cave, it was time to go. Surprisingly, he didn't resist when Charlotte placed him inside the portable cage. Kerry wrangled the big cage into his truck, and it was a tearful good-bye for Charlotte and a cheerful voice for me.

"We're going home, Scarlet, we're going home."

He was quiet on the ride home, pupils wide as he took in the unfamiliar landscape. As we drove up our bumpy driveway, he looked a little concerned, then relieved, to see trees and to hear another bird. With the loss of both Sarah and Zoe, Zachy had become our prime watch bird and the power of his voice had increased. Now Will's pupils constricted as I placed his little cage on the redwood table while Kerry moved the cage into the house. With the daybed gone, the new cage was right in front of the window with a great view to the garden and forest beyond. His old home had had no view; for him, life had been a nine-by-twelve kitchen with a small window that looked out onto a gravel road. With the new cage in place and his food dishes secured, it was showtime.

"Okay, Scarlet, let's go meet the family."

Here he was, the new kid on the block facing a greeting committee. Once out of his little cage, he climbed right up on his familiar one. There, he was the same height as Zach on his perch, and they looked at each other with curiosity. The dogs and cats were mostly uninterested: Been there, done that; just a different color.

"Hello, Will, hello." That was his favorite expression. He had learned it while in the pet store from which Charlotte had "rescued" him for an exorbitant $3,000. Everyone who came in, including the owners, would say that to him incessantly. His only other expression was "Good-bye, Will, good-bye" when everybody left; those two expressions framed his life.

"Good-bye, Will, good-bye!" His wings were raised, his head bobbing up and down, as he looked at Zach across the room. Zach still had no vocabulary, so he simply looked back at him, mystified. Only we humans said good-bye and only when leaving the premises. He must have thought this new bird was a little odd.

"Okay, hon; I have to get out to the job site. I'll see you later tonight."

I had the rest of the morning, the rest of the day, to settle in with the new guy. I blocked out any image or thought of Sarah, focusing only on Will. He was in fact the kind of bird who could become my loving mate—tactile, not vicious, not a flyer. Yes, not a flyer. Even when his clipped wings grew back in, I would never let him out. He would have to be content with the house and the now-enclosed deck. It would be a good life, a safe life.

That day and those that followed saw a quick adjustment on his part. He loved the kibble bits, the almonds, walnuts, and peanuts. He looked forward to fresh fruits and vegetables in the morning and pistachios in the afternoon. In between he savored whatever human food was offered, as did Zach. The routine "one for you and one for him" became a sweet routine. He never tried to bite and taught Zachy not to, either. The dogs didn't mind Scarlet at all. As with Sarah, they learned on day one that the bird ruled. This time Blanco learned without having to get bitten first. The cats looked at me with an expression of no surprise. The new bird couple was going to be just fine. Our family would be whole again.

For me, the overtures of a bird who was not afraid to be touched were truly amazing. Within two days, not only did he step up when asked to, he would also step down. His nails had not been routinely clipped, so my arm was covered with welts and little scratches until I could take him to the vet and have them done properly. I didn't care; he was touching me. When Kerry and I were on the sofa, Will would climb down off his cage and come over to sit in my lap. He had no interest in Kerry, but neither was he aggressive toward him. While Kerry and I watched television, Will would lie on his back in the middle of my lap, allowing me to rub his belly. He also liked having his feet tickled and would move them as if he were riding a bicycle. We tongue-kissed, and he liked to gently tongue my ear and my eyelids. He didn't scream; he wasn't seeking furniture to dine on. I had found the perfect bird.

Within two weeks of his arrival, he had learned new words from listening to me say them over and over again.

"Thank you." "Welcome" (for "You're welcome"). "Love you."

There were also "new" words from his previous ownerships that he had been saving.

"Step up, Will, step up!" "No!" "Bad bird!" Apparently there had been some training glitches. Whenever he said "Bad bird!" I would counter with "Good bird! Good bird!" Eventually the other expression fell away.

He did continue to use the others on Zach. If the little guy didn't respond to whatever Will wanted from him, Will would reprimand him with one of those. Thankfully, he never called him a bad bird.

Kerry was happy that I was happy. The other animals found Will much more agreeable to live with, and our lives were no longer plagued by screaming. Like Sarah, Scarlet followed me around like a dog, climbed everywhere, and loved the fact that he had a deck—now screened in—with more climbing space and many toys: ropes, climbing bars, three madrone perches, stuffed animals, chew toys, and a bell mobile that allowed him to exercise his musical side.

He quickly learned my "leaving" cues: "In my office," "Worky worky," "Trip." I delayed my first New York trip to almost three months after his arrival so that I wouldn't traumatize him.

Zachy bonded with him as with a mate, playing with him and eating next to him; they groomed each other and slept together. Little Zach's plucked feathers began to grow back in; he would be beautiful again.

Friends and family now became regular visitors. Will didn't bite, Zach wasn't aggressive without the nest, which he had abandoned after Zoe flew off, and the two birds together were a source of safe entertainment. When we had parties, Will—and of course Zach—had no desire to go outside, so there was no commotion. When I gardened, Will watched from the deck, not caring that he was not out there with me as long as he could hear or see me. My bird idyll was finally at hand.

The parrot stories that I had been sharing with publishers all these years now took a different turn. Instead of "You won't believe what she did then!" with a tone of exasperation, it became "You won't believe what he did!," this time with the tone of a proud parent recounting her child's newest accomplishment. He was my little genius, my good boy, my loving mate. He was the bird I had always been meant to have.

But what about Sarah and her memory? Four years after her death, I still could not talk about her without becoming tearful. Occasionally, when I walked around our property, I would find one of her wing feathers and tenderly add it to my Sarah collection. When bulbs flowered in the spring, I would think of her digging right there alongside me. Small, unexpected moments would bring me to tears, like the first time Will Scarlet said to me, "Love you." That was the only expression she had ever learned while living with me. Then, of course, in preparation for writing this book I had to reread journal entries and sort through old photos to help bring her alive within these pages. I saved the last three chapters for Labor Day weekend, when I wouldn't have to see anyone; I knew the grief would return, and it did.

I have told her story; I have given her a life beyond her death. In my mind, her spirit still flies among our trees and keeps watch over our roof. She was my first great love and always will be.

EPILOGUE

TODAY OUR PROPERTY looks very different from what it did when Sarah was with us. The garden is more expansive, with a thirty-six-foot-square pond that even has a center moat and a bridge across to it. More neighbors have moved in around us, although they are not in view, and our bucolic little town is becoming more and more a Bay Area "country burb." Kerry continues to build beautiful homes for others; we still live in the trailer. My office cottage now has a minikitchen and a bathroom, so that I can escape from the other house. Our animal population includes Will Scarlet, Zachy, Bug Queen (rescue dog/shar-pei and pit bull), Bodhi (English bulldog), Savvy (Rhodesian ridgeback and pit bull, neighbor's dog who came to visit and wouldn't stay home), Bu-Boy (male cat), Mini-Pak (female cat), and fifty-one very happy koi. Gone are Mistoff and Tiger, both deceased; Ben and Blanco, also deceased; the outside cats, all killed three years ago by a mountain lion who decimated the neighborhood cat population; and Rachel the raccoon with her family.

My life as an agent is much less complicated than when Sarah was here; my powers of concentration are not diminished by screams and dissonance. I am now an author, in addition to maintaining a small client base, and am more active in our community theater group, for which I have directed three plays. I garden more, reflect more, and see my life as a wonderful balance among work, play, and personal, spiritual growth.

Sarah

Sarah taught me much. She taught me about unbounded potential and new limits. She taught me about tolerance. She taught me that dreams cannot, must not, be mitered about the corners. She taught me about my own mother and her frailties, which I all too often perceived as flaws. Ultimately, she taught me about love.

RESOURCES

Any novice in search of a parrot, especially a macaw, needs solid information before committing to the demands of such a bird. Even those who already have such a bird can benefit from additional perspectives and recommendations. The resources included in this section will help readers get that information before welcoming a large parrot (macaw, cockatoo, African grey) into their lives and/or help in the relationship with their current bird.

The first section, General Organizations, offers listings of associations and clubs whose scope includes multiple species. The second section, Specific Species, looks at African greys, cockatoos, conures, and macaws. Certainly, there are many parrot species to choose from, but these four—because of their size and variable temperament—are most relevant to my experience with a macaw. The third and final section, Bird Rescue Organizations, identifies national and international groups whose mission is to save parrots in distress, often helping to place the rescued bird in a safe home. Readers can also check for listings in their own state by using a search engine like Google or Yahoo! and the keywords bird rescue, parrot rescue, macaw rescue, cockatoo rescue, or African grey rescue. Avian veterinarians (Association of Avian Veterinarians) are also an excellent source of information about parrots; many of these medical doctors are also bird owners or breeders. Additionally, local clubs exist in many states, usually found under the heading "Parrot Club." In addition to being a source of information and support, these local clubs are a good source for obtaining a parrot. Pet stores in general should be checked out with a local avian veterinarian or club familiar with their selling stock.

Zachy and Will Scarlet

Ultimately, just as parents do with other parents, parrot owners need to connect with other parrot owners, who can help enrich and protect the human/parrot relationship. Local veterinarians and clubs can help create these connections.

General Organizations

American Federation of Aviculture (AFA)
www.afa.birds.org/index.html

The AFA comprises more than two hundred affiliated bird clubs and organizations representing more than fifty thousand aviculturists.

Association of Avian Veterinarians
www.aav.org

This professional organization is dedicated to advancing and promoting avian medicine and care. It also has listings of avian veterinarians in your area.

Avian Protection Society
www.avianprotectors.homestead.com

The Avian Protection Society focuses on problems facing captive birds. It offers referrals to avian rescue organizations and advice on avian issues.

Avian Publications
www.avianpublications.com

For more than thirty years, Avian Publications has produced the finest books and videos on bird keeping, care, training, and breeding, along with classic avian references. Species covered include African greys, macaws, cockatoos, and conures.

Avian Web: The Bird Lover's Resource
www.avianweb.com

This website has the latest information on parrot basics, bird care and husbandry, bird health care, and bird diseases and research.

Avian Welfare Coalition
www.avianwelfare.org

The AWC is an alliance of veterinarians, conservationists, and avian welfare and animal protection organizations dedicated to the ethical treatment of parrots and other captive exotic birds.

Avicultural Society of America
www.asabirds.org

Founded in 1927, the society promotes the study of foreign and native birds, education on the care, breeding, and feeding of birds, and the preservation of endangered bird species.

Exotic Bird Breeders Association of America
www.keyinfo.com/bird/pages/ebbaa/ebbaa.html

Good information for prospective parrot owners and for those who already have a parrot. It also publishes the journal *Breeders' Bulletin.*

International Aviculturists Society
www.funnyfarmexotics.com/IAS/

This group of aviculturists from around the world strives to protect, preserve, and enhance the keeping and breeding of all exotic birds.

North American Parrot Society
www.northamericanparrotsociety.com

The society is a nonprofit organization dedicated to educating members about all species of parrots, improving show standards, and putting fun and fairness into showing birds. Members include private owners, breeders, and veterinarians.

Parrot Association of Canada
www.parrotscanada.org

Aviculturists and breeders with an interest in the preservation of parrot species and other avian species joined together to create this association. It has much information on proper avian husbandry techniques for aviculturists and the general public.

Parrot Chronicles
www.parrotchronicles.com

This online magazine has photographs and stories from real parrot lovers and is a good source of information about health, behavior, and care.

Parrot House
www.parrothouse.com

Sam Foster is an avian consultant who specializes in cockatoo care and behavior. This site has many articles by her, "dedicated to helping others understand the behavior and complexities of the birds she loves best."

Parrot Preservation Society
www.parrotpro.com

This site has many informative articles about the care, housing, transportation, and breeding of macaws, cockatoos, Amazons, and conures.

Parrots as Pets
www.parrots-as-pets.com

This new advice blog for owners of African greys, Amazons, and macaws has loads of information on various species, parrot accessories, parrot diet, and parrot training.

Pet Bird by Up at Six Aviaries
www.upatsix.com

This is the ultimate avian page on the Internet. It has listings for avian associations and online suppliers of food, treats, toys, and cages; listings to find your special bird; a gallery of avian artwork; resources on avian behavior; listings of avian sanctuaries for rescue and adoption; online chat groups; and many articles on avian issues.

Real Macaw Parrot Club
www.realmacaw.com

This all-species parrot club has a monthly newsletter, book and tape lending library, grooming demonstrations, educational programs, and fund-raising for avian medical research and conservation projects.

Society of Parrot Breeders and Exhibitors
www.spbe.org

This international society promotes excellence in captive breeding programs and education for aviculturists on the proper management and care of all parrots.

Tropical Rainforest Coalition
www.rainforest.org

Since many parrot species originate in tropical rain forests, this site helps parrot owners better understand the birds' environmental needs.

The True Parrot
www.thetrueparrot.homestead.com

This site provides valuable information for new and potential parrot guardians to enhance the life of parrots in captivity. The True Parrot covers parrots' social needs, diet and nutrition, veterinary needs, and housing.

World Parrot Trust
www.worldparrottrust.org

Online encyclopedia and reference library, blogs, and the latest information about endangered parrots, the illegal parrot trade, and parrot conservation efforts made by groups around the globe.

Specific Species

AFRICAN GREY

An African Grey
www.anafricangrey.ca

Many articles on behavior, health and nutrition, training, and rehabilitation make this a standout site. There are also do-it-yourself projects and recipes for your grey's special dietary needs.

African Grey Parrot
www.theafricangreyparrot.com

This practical site has a guide to choosing the best cage for your parrot, recommendations for a healthy diet, and the Grey Forum, where you can post questions and get a quick response.

African Grey Parrot Info
http://africangreyparrot.info

Apart from having a popular forum at http://vdnent.proboards41.com, the site also offers free personal grey blogs and a grey gallery. The site, managed by Dandy, has information on nutrition, behavior, training, diet, and medical care. Dandy also has a diary, sound files, and pictures available.

African Grey Parrots
www.africancongogrey.com

For the owner who wants to know about diet and how to train his or her bird; includes a list of suggested books.

Africangreys.com
www.africangreys.com

This site has many articles on how to care for your bird, nutrition advice, and living-together skills. The Grey Play Round Table Online information center and grey expert Maggie Wright are especially helpful.

The Alex Foundation
www.alexfoundation.org

Alex the Grey could identify objects by their names, shapes, and colors and was the most advanced example of an animal's comprehension of the English language. He passed away in September 2007 at the age of thirty-one. The Alex Foundation supports research to expand the base of knowledge establishing the cognitive and communicative abilities of parrots as intelligent beings. It encourages the responsible ownership of parrots, conservation and preservation of parrots in the wild, and veterinary research into the psychological diseases and care of these birds.

Grey Forums
www.greyforums.net

This online resource for African greys has articles about understanding your grey, health and nutrition, news, links to other sites, information about products, blogs, and access to community experts.

Wings Central
www.wingscentral.org/aps

The society makes available information, articles, and pictures of African parrots: greys, vasas, and the Poicephalus species (Meyer's, Senegal, cape, and Jardine's).

COCKATOO

Cockatoo Birds
www.cockatoo-birds.com

This site has information on life span, housing, and social structure and links for the prospective and present cockatoo owner.

Cockatoo Street
www.cockatoostreet.com

For those interested in having a cockatoo as a companion, this site has information on issues such as commitment, tips for a happy bird, the housework involved, and adoption.

Moluccan Cockatoo Society
www.moluccancockatoo.org

The society maintains a site with information about cockatoos as pets, in the wild, a pronunciation guide to "moluccan," fan sites, and memorials.

My Toos
www.mytoos.com

This opinionated site promises "Everything you never wanted to know about cockatoos—and what they won't tell you." There are a cockatoo article library, message board, letters, rescue information, and announcements.

Umbrella Cockatoo
www.theumbrellacockatoo.com

Bonus the umbrella cockatoo has his own site, loaded with practical information about cockatoos' needs. Articles on diet, toys, and grooming and a photo gallery of Bonus are included.

CONURE

The Conure Community
www.conurecommunity.com

Conure lovers come together here to discuss topics of interest and share stories and information about their birds.

International Conure Association
www.conure.org

This site has an information center, news about conservation projects, a store, and reprints from the *ICA Journal.*

Nanday Conure Page
www.nanday.com

Nanday owners are encouraged to contribute photos, stories, and multimedia files of their birds. There are a message board, an annotated list of nanday conure home pages, links to general nanday conure information, and frequently asked questions about these birds.

Sun Conures
www.sunconureparrots.com

This site is dedicated to sun conure diet and nutrition, as well as training and behavior.

www.concentric.net/~Conure/conures.shtml

Linda loves her conure, Louie, and maintains a website of almost every bit of information a conure owner needs to ensure the health and happiness of his or her bird.

www.z11.invisionfree.com/Conure_Crazy/

This active forum has information on health, feeding, and training for conure owners and anyone with an interest in these birds.

MACAW

All About Macaws
www.allaboutmacaws.com

Jessica Harrison, known as "The Macaw Maniac," has a free e-newsletter that includes a comprehensive list of foods, tips on getting to know your macaw better, and grooming for different breeds. She addresses common health problems and prevention and how to exercise your macaw.

Macaw Landing Foundation
www.macawlanding.org

The foundation is a conservation organization dedicated to the preservation of macaws. Its interests include the propagation of endangered macaws, wildlife management, and environmental education, as well as building public awareness and supporting other organizations that work to preserve macaws in the wild.

Macaw Parrots
www.macaw-parrots.com

This site lists the seventeen species of macaws and provides information for the macaw owner from behavioral problems to diet.

All About the Magnificent Macaw
www.magnificentmacaws.com

This site, which concentrates on macaw behavior problems, has dozens of articles about training macaws, a training newsletter, and access to training videos.

Those Majestic Macaws
www.exoticbird.com

This fun resource is for macaw owners and anyone with an interest in macaws. It has a disclaimer that the information is contributed by people with an interest in macaws and is not intended to be expert advice.

Bird Rescue Organizations

Avian Education Rescue & Adoption Services (AERAS)
www.aeras-parrots.org

Besides rescue and adoption, AERAS provides educational resources for basic and advanced care of parrots and other exotic birds.

Bird Placement Program Parrot Refuge
www.avi-sci.com/bpp/

This program offers parrot refuge and rescue, plus adoption of unwanted parrots. It also provides assistance with bird care, behavior problems, and parrot nutrition and an online bird magazine.

Center for Avian Adoption, Rescue, and Education (CAARE)
www.caare.net

The center is always seeking qualified homes for its foster and adoption programs. Careful consideration is given on a case-by-case basis to the parrot and the prospective adoptive family, and to placing the right parrot in the right home.

Feathered Family
www.featheredfamily.com

Feathered Family is an exotic birds rescue organization in Colorado that helps parrots find loving homes.

Feathered Friends Avian Rescue
www.parrotrescue.ca

This Canadian organization is devoted to the rescue and care of unwanted parrots and to finding them stable, loving homes.

Foster Parrots
www.fosterparrots.com

This rescue, adoption, and sanctuary facility is dedicated to improving the lives of all parrots by providing the truth about the difficulties of keeping a parrot healthy and happy. Foster Parrots is a member of the Avian Welfare Coalition.

Fresh Start Bird Rescue
www.freshstart4pets.petfinder.com

Dedicated to finding permanent homes for parrots who have found themselves homeless, this site also includes many articles about parrot care, feeding, and training.

Greyhaven Exotic Bird Sanctuary
www.greyhaven.bc.ca

Greyhaven specializes in parrot rescue, refuge, and adoptions, and has rehabilitation and education programs for exotic birds.

HealthiPet Network Corporation
www.pbcompanies.com/healthipets/

The name is an acronym for "Helping Endangered Animals Lives Through Interstate Placement Evaluations & Teachings." This nonprofit operates a no-kill shelter and places companions in homes outside their area or home state.

Knapptime Adoption, Rescue, and Education
www.knapp-time.com

Knapptime helps unwanted or rescued companion birds find loving homes with people who are experienced in bird care or eager to learn.

Midwest Avian Adoption and Rescue Services (MAARS)
www.maars.org

Serving the Midwest, MAARS provides education for people who live with pet birds and rescue, foster care, adoption, and sanctuary placement for companion birds in need. MAARS is a member of the Avian Welfare Coalition.

National Parrot Rescue and Preservation Society
www.parrotfestival.org

The nonprofit society promotes an annual Parrot Festival in Houston, Texas. It provides information to other rescue organizations on the capture and care of parrots and actively seeks qualified homes for parrots.

Parrot Rehabilitation Society
www.parrotsociety.org

The society takes in homeless, unwanted, or abused parrots and finds them permanent, loving homes with its members. It also provides education about the special needs of these birds and promotes good health and enriched lives for feathered companions.

Parrot Education and Adoption Center (PEAC)
www.peac.org

The Parrot Education and Adoption Center is a nonprofit, volunteer organization dedicated to educating current and potential bird owners on the proper care of pet birds. Unwanted or found parrots are accepted at PEAC and are cared for until adopted by qualified applicants.

Parrots First
www.parrotsfirst.org

This rescue and adoption service helps unwanted or found parrots find new homes and holds many educational classes and seminars.

Parrots-R-4Ever
www.parrotsr4ever.org

This no-kill rescue shelter and sanctuary provides care, rehabilitation, and adoption services for exotic pet birds.

Raven's Haven Exotic Bird Rescue
www.ravenshaven.org

Raven's Haven rescues unwanted parrots and acts as a placement service for friendly, tame birds. It also serves as an educational resource for prospective and present parrot owners. Raven's Haven is a member of the Avian Welfare Coalition.

Safe Haven Avian Placement Services
www.safehavenfl.org

This organization provides rescue, rehabilitation, education, and adoption services to ensure lifelong enrichment for the companion bird experience.

Second Chance Bird Rescue and Rehabilitation
www.secondchancebirdrescue.com

Second Chance rehabilitates birds with behavior issues and helps find them homes and loving families.

'Too Haven Cockatoo Rescue and Adoption
www.toohaven.org

'Too Haven rehabilitates rescued cockatoos and places them in permanent homes. It provides education and educational resources for present and potential parrot owners, including diet and care requirements.

ACKNOWLEDGMENTS

I WANT FIRST TO THANK my truly gifted editor, Julia Pastore, whose "exterior eye" profoundly helped transform my "interior eye" and inspired a more dramatic rendering of my experience. Julia is rare indeed. Next, I send loving hugs to my dear friend, author, painter, and Random House legend Toinette Lippe. It was she who first said, "This is a book." Another round of deep appreciation goes to the entire Harmony group, including Kate Kennedy, who was always available. And of course, the highest gratitude to Shaye Areheart and Jenny Frost for saying "Yes."

Will Scarlet

In order of support and encouragement, I wish to thank the following people: my husband, Kerry, for his unconditional belief in my ability to fly; my secretary and dear friend, Maureen Moore, whose attention to detail helped bring this book to life; my diligent associate and good friend, Sal Glynn, without whose help I could never have made my manuscript deadline; my dear friend Mary Bulles, who has always seen me as a spirit mother; Leeya Thompson, another dear friend and my former agency office manager, who has always believed that I knew how to fly; my sister, Susan Ellis-Good, who has continued to remind me that I know how to write; my nieces, Jessica Dhaliwal, Jennifer Dhaliwal, Lisa Dhaliwal, and Meghan Dhaliwal, who believe my relationship with animals is special; all of my teachers over the years who taught me how to love language; Robert Bly, who after reviewing my poetry told me that I had a powerful voice; Wayne Root, for his remarkable spiritual gift; Andrea Brown, the "Buddhiva" who stood by me in both good and difficult times; Lori Pingrey, whose devotion to my animals allowed me to travel for business; and Stephanie Chatten, for all of her amazing gifts.

There are many other individuals who in some way contributed to the birthing of this book. To all of you, a heartfelt thank-you.

Finally, I thank Sarah, who was my greatest teacher and within whom flew the spirit of my mother; my father would have been proud. And very last, I thank all the spirits, muses, and animal presences who led me to this story. My gratitude to all.

Will Scarlet

ABOUT THE AUTHOR

With Sarah

NANCY ELLIS-BELL is a recognized literary agent, former professor, and author. Dividing her time between her mountain home in northern California and New York, she has been active in the publishing business for thirty years. Raised in San Francisco, she holds a master's degree in literature along with extensive postgraduate units in psychology. Awards include national writing grants, faculty distinction, and recognition by *Writer's Digest* as one of the top twenty-five agents in the country. Animals have been her passion since childhood; her introduction to the world of exotic birds started eleven years ago and has taken that passion to life-changing levels. During this time, she has adopted or rescued three macaws, including her current scarlet macaw, Will Scarlet, and three conures, two of them wild-caught, and has helped to find homes for several other birds. Her family is rounded out by three dogs, two cats, fifty-one koi, and a husband who understands her passion. Visit her at TheBarkingParrot.com.